Through the Leaves
and Other Plays

FRANZ XAVER KROETZ

Through the Leaves and Other Plays

TRANSLATED BY ROGER DOWNEY

TCG TRANSLATIONS

Through the Leaves and Other Plays is published by Theatre Communications Group, Inc., 355 Lexington Ave., New York, NY 10017.

TCG gratefully acknowledges public funds from the National Endowment for the Arts, the New York State Council on the Arts and the New York City Department of Cultural Affairs in addition to the generous support of the following foundations and corporations: Alcoa Foundation, Ameritech Foundation, ARCO Foundation, AT&T Foundation, Consolidated Edison Company of New York, Council of Literary Magazines and Presses, Nathan Cummings Foundation, Dayton Hudson Foundation, Ford Foundation, GTE, James Irvine Foundation, Jerome Foundation, Management Consultants for the Arts, Andrew W. Mellon Foundation, Metropolitan Life Foundation, National Broadcasting Company, Pew Charitable Trusts, Philip Morris Companies Inc., Scherman Foundation, Shubert Foundation, L. J. Skaggs and Mary C. Skaggs Foundation, Lila Wallace-Reader's Digest Fund.

Kroetz, Franz Xaver, 1946-
[Plays. English. Selections]
Through the leaves and other plays / Franz Xaver Kroetz : translated by Roger Downey.
— 1st ed.
(TCG Translations 1)
Contents: Through the leaves — Mensch meier — The nest.
ISBN 1-55936-044-5 (cloth) — ISBN 1-55936-043-7 (paper)
1. Kroetz, Franz Xaver, 1946- —Translations, English.
I. Downey, Roger. II. Kroetz, Franz Xaver, 1946- Wer durchs Laub geht. English. 1992.
III. Kroetz, Franz Xaver, 1946- Mensch Meier. English. 1992. IV. Kroetz, Franz Xaver,
1946- Nest. English. 1992. V. Title. VI. Series.
PT2671.R59A24–1992

832'.914—dc20   92-3954
                                                                                                        CIP

Cover design and watercolor copyright © 1992 by Barry Moser
Design and composition by The Sarabande Press
Color separations provided by EMR Systems Communication

First Edition, July 1992

ISBN 978-1-63670-159-2

CONTENTS

Introduction

Franz Xaver Kroetz turned 46 this year. Like the three-year-older Sam Shepard—the American playwright whose career Kroetz's own most nearly resembles—he is hardly a figure for the history books yet. But—again like Shepard—whatever direction Kroetz takes in future, the works in this volume, written at about four-year intervals between 1969 and 1981, will remain among those that define world drama in the 1970s. Although the three plays in this volume are free-standing works, they also form part of a kind of dramatic cycle. No unprejudiced reader is likely to deny their power; but for their originality fully to be appreciated, they must be seen in the context in which they were created.

The same very much applies to their author, because in many ways Kroetz began as, and remains today, something of an outsider: a cuckoo in the nest of German *Kultur*.

He was born in 1946, the son of a government tax official. Apparently an indifferent student in elementary school, he was routed by the rigid Bavarian examination system and family pressure into a kind of tradeschool-business college devoted to turning out junior employees for government and corporate use. At 15, he flunked out: a catastrophic event in the life of a respectable German family, hard to conceive for anyone growing up under looser American educational conditions.

Kroetz decided that he wanted to become an actor, and after three years' conservatory training got his certificate of competency. But even in the highly organized German training system, a certificate does not guarantee a job, and for the next six years, Kroetz spent much of his time in casual labor: in a paper warehouse, as a chauffeur, hospital orderly, newspaper deliveryman.

He also from time to time worked at various amateur and "alternative" theatres, including the late Rainer Werner Fassbinder's Munich "antitheater." For a time he served as a utility actor in unpretentious Bavarian-dialect farces at the Ludwig Thoma Theater in a resort town in the foothills of the Alps south of Munich—"playing everything, the 17-year-old farmboy who's always getting clipped on the ear to the 63-year-old farmer who wants to get married just one more time."

During this period of apprenticeship—as early as 1966—Kroetz began to write. His was an unconventional background for a budding German playwright. Few "serious" German authors have failed to attend university, where they are pumped full of German literary tradition and its attendant literary class-system, its implicit gradations from *Dichter* to *Schriftsteller* down to *Journalist*.

Left-wing German literary circles decry such distinctions, but the system left its marks on the prose and attitudes of its graduates nonetheless. Kroetz came to theatre directly, not via the academy, free of the burden of upholding, or even struggling to cast off, the 200-year-old tradition of the playwright as spokesman for eternal verities.

The highly institutionalized civic and state theatre system of West Germany also has its formative effects on those who work within it. A man who loves independence, Kroetz was fortunate in his birthplace. Munich is one of the very few cities in West

Germany where a lively "free-theater" scene exists and thrives. Like his compatriot and exact contemporary Rainer Werner Fassbinder, Kroetz was free to develop his craft in his own wayward fashion, free to act, direct, write as he pleased, paying little regard to "the Culture Industry" as embodied in the vast production machines of the state-subsidized companies.

By the time Kroetz arrived at maturity in the late Sixties, those machines were beginning to creak dangerously. The postwar German theatre had been explicitly designed as a sanctuary, a place devoted to the classics, to Goethe and Schiller, to Shakespeare, Shaw and Sophocles, to the "poetic realism" of Williams and Miller, the enameled fancies of Giradoux and Fry. If critical attitudes to contemporary society were expressed at all, it was allegorically, through the neo-Expressionism of writers like the Swiss authors Frisch and Dürrenmatt. But by the mid-Sixties, a post-war generation full of nothing but contempt for *Kultur* and its smug consumers was ready to take on contemporary reality again. In Franz Xaver Kroetz they found a dramatist eager not only to portray reality, but rub his audience's nose in it.

All the most striking characteristics of Kroetzian dramaturgy appear already fully-formed in the earliest play in the published canon: *Game Crossing*, which dates from 1968. The play's 27 short scenes occur in more than a dozen locations centering on a crowded working-class family apartment. Scenes begin and end sharply, abruptly—once Kroetz uses the theatrical equivalent of a jump-cut with particularly telling effect—but within each scene the timing and texture are those of the most minuscule kitchen sink realism: people take showers, use the toilet, eat meals, wash dishes, shop, picnic, make love, work, tell dirty jokes. The dialogue is couched in the most ordinary of ordinary language, broken by half-completed sentences and desultory silences.

The author's notes on performing style in *Game Crossing* are exemplary for virtually all his later work. "The baldness (*Karg-*

heit) of the language should be matched by an economy in the stage picture. Projections could be used to sketch in the various realistic settings quickly and simply. Alternatively I recommend a bare stage with only the most essential set pieces." The cast of *Game Crossing* is equally exemplary: a truckdriver, his wife and teenaged daughter, and the daughter's boyfriend. (Six other figures appear briefly: in later Kroetz pieces the number of characters is pared down as ruthlessly as the language and settings, to the bare minimum necessary to the action.)

In plays set in Austrian hill-towns, on remote Bavarian farms, in urban high-rise apartments, the same types recur again and again: truckdrivers, *Hausfrauen*, half-grown children, common laborers, facing again and again the same situations: lack of money, lack of a job, family frictions, unwanted babies, trouble with the cops, the boss, the neighbors. In a sympathetic essay in the 1978 season-end wrap-up issue of the German periodical *Theater heute*, critic Michael Skasa remarked ("quite without irony, quite in earnest") that after repeated readings of more than 15 of Kroetz's plays, "I can't remember who is married to whom, which ones have a child already and which still don't own a car, who's got a color TV and whose apartment is too small. . . . Kroetz puts the reality of the group of human beings before us. The group is very large, the differences between its members very slight."

The reality depicted in all Kroetz's earlier work is penetrated through and through with violence and the threat of violence. Some German critics found the plays melodramatic, even sensationalistic, and certainly there is hardly a piece before 1974 without its rape, abortion, baby-murder or suicide, its half-wit, cripple or fumbling petty criminal. To an American familiar with the popular dramatic literature of the 1930s, the Kroetzian milieu may recall that of John Steinbeck—or, even less flatteringly, Erskine Caldwell.

But even Kroetz's earliest plays are devoid of the sentimen-
tality, the romantic idealization of poverty and ignorance, that
make *Of Mice and Men* or *God's Little Acre* such queasy reading
today. In early Kroetz, a flat, hard light beats down on everything,
for characters and audience alike: there are no shadows to creep
into, no corners to hide in. The characters are so rigidly confined
by circumstance, by character, by the very language they speak,
that violence seems only the natural outcome of unbearable pressure. In these early plays, political or social criticism is entirely
implicit: a society capable of producing the stunted, half-timid,
half-ferocious figures that populate them must *ipso facto* be rotten,
root and branch.

In 1973, Kroetz was the most-performed living playwright in
the German language, but found himself at something of a dead
end in his work. He began striking out in new and controversial
directions. Always the maverick, he joined the fearfully un-
fashionable Deutsche Kommunistische Partei—the most conven-
tional and doctrinaire of left-wing West German parties, with
strong liaisons to the ruling Sozialistische Einheitspartei of East
Germany. Most of his time over the next year and a half was
devoted to reportage and adversary journalism. When after more
than a year Kroetz wrote his next straight play for the stage, he
returned to the form and milieu of the earlier plays but with a
different attitude toward his materials.

The Nest, written in 1974, premiered in 1975, is a free-standing
work, but also a kind of commentary on an earlier play: the two-
character *Upper Austria*, written in 1972. To make sure no one
misses the connection, Kroetz takes extreme measures. Not only
are the characters of *The Nest*, sociologically speaking, identical
with those of the earlier piece: the two plays begin with an
identical situation—a couple sitting in their living room at the
end of an evening of TV.

But *The Nest* begins with a warm, impersonal voice on the TV

announcing "You've been watching . . . *Upper Austria*: a play by
the Bavarian author Franz Xaver Kroetz." What's more, Kurt and
Martha casually discuss the play they've seen before going to bed,
even making some elementary connections between its story and
their own situation. Such self-consciousness, such awareness of
the possibility that things can be different than they are, would
have been far beyond the capacities of the dreamy, feckless Heinz
and Anni of the earlier play.

Upper Austria is, among the early plays, strikingly placid in
event. Truckdriver Heinz does *not* murder his pregnant wife; Anni
does *not* get a backstairs abortion. But the play provides little
reason to expect the couple's future to be brighter than their past:
the play ends as it began, with dreams of a trip to Vienna,
accompanied by a Strauss waltz wheezed out on a concertina.

Martha and Kurt in *The Nest* are not dreamers but, however
fumblingly, doers, and the sphere of their activity is meticulously
defined. In the third scene of the first act Kurt and Martha spend
a long Saturday afternoon calculating the cost of having a baby.
The text of the scene is little more than a catalog of nursery items,
brand names and prices; but before it is over we know not only the
precise economic situation of the little family but also its members' attitudes to the outside world and their perceptions of self:
Martha's fiscal naivete and TV-commercial-cultivated "consum-
erism," Kurt's paternal attitude to his wife and his dependence on
the boss's continued favor, the couple's unquestioning submission
to the rule of "keeping up with the neighbors."

The Nest is also novel in the intimate linkage established between the private lives of the characters and a specific external
condition that concerns society-at-large. Partly through ignorance, partly through a stubborn refusal to face inconvenient
facts, Kurt makes himself responsible for (literally) poisoning his
private Paradise, a little Alpine lake, and thereby for the illness of
his baby son. In accepting that responsibility, Kurt implicitly

accepts responsibility for his own life. The individual does not make the world he lives in; but any change in that world begins with an individual choice. The play ends with Kurt's decision to be no longer, in his own words, "a trained ape" in someone else's circus.

The Nest is a transitional work in Kroetz's *oeuvre*. The private and public worlds of the play make contact but do not, so to speak, interpenetrate, and the manner in which contact is brought about seems a little mechanical, if only in comparison to the seamless dramaturgy of the "private" scenes in the play. Three years later, *Mensch Meier*, described by the author as the completion of a trilogy with *Upper Austria* and *The Nest*, had its simultaneous premiere at four West German theaters. It is difficult not to regard the play as Kroetz's masterpiece.

In this tale of a jittery, imaginative Munich assembly-line worker, his vague, housebound wife, and their silently observant teenage son, he has achieved an almost perfect blending of a family microcosm and societal macrocosm, finding ways to deploy the action on the largest emotional and thematic scale without violating his own strict canons of verisimilitude.

The development of Kroetz's worldview and dramaturgy during the 1970s is easy to discern through a comparative reading of the successive versions of the dramatic material first published as *Men's Business* in 1970. This first portrayal of the relationship between a female butcher and her laborer lover ends with a scene of expressionistic violence. The final version, *Through the Leaves*, first performed in 1981, begins with identical characters and an identical situation; but the development of the action reflects an enormous maturation both in social understanding and in subtlety of dramatic technique.

In the decade from 1968 to 1978, Kroetz wrote over 20 full-length and one-act plays for theatre, radio and television. After 1978, that explosive productivity slowed dramatically. Having explored his dramatic home ground so thoroughly, the author had to cast further afield for fresh material, both thematically and conceptually. *Neither Fish nor Fowl* (1981) portrayed two couples more rootless-urban than displaced-rural, more young Ludwig Meier's generation than father Otto's. *Fear and Hope of the Federal Republic of Germany*, subtitled "Scenes from everyday German life in the year 1983," was a cavalcade of brief, disconnected, snapshot-vivid scenes all portraying one way or another the dislocations brought on by the slackening of the economy. *Farmers Die* (1985) was the most radical departure yet; a phantasmagoric fairy tale/horror story set "somewhere between Landshut and Calcutta."

Kroetz spent far more of his time in the late Eighties performing, directing, adapting (Ernst Toller's World War One casualty drama, *der deutsche Hinkemann*; Goncharov's novel *Oblomov*) and acting than at his writing desk. His most recently-produced work, *Farmer Theater*, which had its world-premiere in Cologne in April 1991, is an extravagant, quasi-autobiographical, quasi-hallucinatory compression of the unproduced, previously published book-length "drama," *The Author as Swine*.

In a way it's not surprising that Kroetz, in the early work the most self-effacing of authors, has made his own life the subject of his latest writing. Through performing his own works on tour and on television, he was already a modest national celebrity when he was cast in 1988 as the decadent, corrupt gossip columnist Baby Schimmerlos in the television mini-series, *Kir Royale*.

This lurid, *Dynasty*-derived, six-part satirical stroll through contemporary Munich cafe society turned the author from literary celebrity to media superstar. Again like Shepard, Kroetz's life, opinions and above all romantic liaisons are now grist for tabloid cover stories. And the author has not been averse to cashing in on the publicity. A series of tendentious columns written for the politically-conservative *Bild-Zeitung* have put Kroetz irremediably beyond the acceptable pale with the politically correct, formerly his greatest fans. *Farmer Theater* has been read by such observers as a cry of encoded self-loathing by a formerly serious writer who's sold out to success.

It can also be read—and was so presented in Torsten Fischer's slick, speedy, strident Cologne premiere—as Kroetz's *Day of the Locust*, a no-holds-barred, no-prisoners-taken confessional-confrontational summing-up of one man's headfirst encounter with capital-S Success in contemporary Germany. One thing is certain about the piece; without familiarity with the historical, social and personal context within which it was written, the play is well-nigh incomprehensible to North Americans, while the quieter, more mundane world of the earlier plays is still capable of engaging us and drawing us in. Already, less than a generation after their composition, they're beginning to look very much like classics, and their apparently ingenuous "realism" like the superlative craft of a theatre poet.

—Roger Downey

Through
The Leaves

Wer durchs Laub geht, muss das Rauschen dulden.

If you go walking through the leaves,
you'll have to put up with the rustling . . .

—Bavarian proverb

This translation was made from the 1979 Suhrkamp edition of *Wer durchs Laub geht* . . . The play was first copyrighted in 1976.

Through the Leaves is the fourth version of material first treated in *Man's Work* (*Männersache*). Written in 1970, first performed in 1972, published in 1973, *Männersache* ends with an almost expressionistically extreme scene of double murder/suicide. *Männersache* and one of its revisions, *Ein Mann ein Wörterbuch*, have been published in English, as *Men's Business* and *A Man, a Dictionary*, in *Farmyard and Four Other Plays* (Urizen Books, 1976). *Through the Leaves* is presumably Kroetz's last word on this material.

The German text of *Through the Leaves* contains no notes on setting or characters. The descriptive material included in this edition is taken from *Männersache*. Where necessary I have added supplementary material in brackets. Martha's dog, which does not actually appear onstage in *Through the Leaves*, is described in *Männersache* as "a mongrel shepherd dog."

Kroetz does not indicate how the selections from Martha's diary are to be performed. In the American productions to date, the directors have selected a mixture of live and recorded presentation.

The German text is not divided into acts. In the Empty Space production an act break was inserted after Scene 4: "Otto is back again. At last." Other productions have been played without intermission.

3

Martha, the cat's-meat-seller. She is between 30 and
40 years old, dark-haired, moderately ugly;
usually wears a butcher's smock.

Otto, a worker (*Eisenflechter*) about 40 years old, average.
[Note Scene 2, where he appears to work indoors on some
kind of packing line. Construction worker would seem to fit
better with his casual working habits.]

SETTING

A utility-meat butcher shop consisting of the shop itself, a
small adjoining room, farther back the walk-in cooler, also
imagined toward the back a small garden; the entry door
to one side. To be constructed as a unit set to avoid scene
changes. [*Through the Leaves* requires in addition spaces
corresponding to the living room, bedroom and
bathroom of Martha's upstairs living quarters.]

SCENE ONE

In the room next to the shop. After closing. Clatter of dishes and cutlery.
A dog is howling outside.

MARTHA *(Giggling)*: Bottoms up!

Martha and Otto drink.

OTTO: This is pretty fancy.

MARTHA: When you're with me you know you been
somewhere. I do pretty well for myself. That's caviar
there, a little tiny jar costs three marks eighty.

OTTO: Caviar! . . . Tastes like fish.

MARTHA: That's what it is, fish eggs.

OTTO: Little eggs.

MARTHA: These fish, they lay millions of eggs like that. You
got to put some butter on top, that brings out the flavor.

OTTO: Living like a king!

MARTHA: This is nothing, you can't fix anything nice in the

shop. You come home with me sometime, you'll see what I can do! *(Smiles to herself)*

OTTO: This ain't your Russian caviar, though, right?

MARTHA: No. *(Short pause)* It's German, what else. You can just stick to the sausage, you don't like it.

OTTO: It's fine, just the Russian is better.

MARTHA: Have you ever really eaten real Russian caviar?

OTTO: You just know stuff like that.

Short pause.

MARTHA: Well I like it. *(Pause)* If you hadn't come tonight I was going to go to the movies.

OTTO: What's on?

MARTHA: *Ben Hur*. It's an old movie I saw ten years ago but really unforgettable. Did you see it too?

OTTO: No.

MARTHA: Do you know the story?

OTTO: I said I didn't see it.

MARTHA: You want me to just tell you quick what it's about?

OTTO: Not interested.

MARTHA *(Laughs)*: OK. *(Pause)* If you don't want any more, just say so, I'll clear up.

OTTO: All done, take her away.

MARTHA: You don't want any more?

OTTO: King in the morning, keep a store at noon, beggar in the evening, old too soon.

MARTHA: All right, I'll clear up. *(Clatter of cutlery and crockery)* I just started doing something I never done before.

OTTO: What's that?

MARTHA: Three guesses.

OTTO: No thanks.

MARTHA: Because you'd never be able to. *(Short pause)* A diary!

Otto laughs.

Really! *(Gropes in her bag)* There. You can read what I wrote in it already.

OTTO: What, a love story?

MARTHA: I wrote about you.

OTTO: What'd you write about me?

MARTHA: That you come into my life, that's what. Go ahead and read it, you'll see.

OTTO: Hunh! *(Laughs)*

MARTHA: You can read everything I wrote. I don't have any secrets from you.

OTTO: 'Cause I can see right through you.

MARTHA: You got to hold on to the good things you come up against in life, then you've got something to look back on.

OTTO: I was no good in Composition.

MARTHA: Oh, I was. Because I got a lot of imagination.

OTTO: Me too. Only not the kind where you want to write it all down.

MARTHA: What kind then?

OTTO: Maybe I'll tell you sometime. If you're good. Not now, though.

MARTHA: Suit yourself. Should I write something into it right now? *(Short pause)* So it won't be forgotten?

OTTO: Showing off.

MARTHA: I know what. *(She writes in her book)*

OTTO: Everybody to his own taste. *(He gropes around in his briefcase and takes out a magazine)*

MARTHA: What's that?

OTTO: Nothing; for men only.

MARTHA: Nothing but naked women!

OTTO: None of your business, keep on writing.

MARTHA: I want to see what's in there. . . . I like this one the best.

OTTO: Average. There's better.

MARTHA: Are they whores who let people take naked pictures of them?

OTTO: Shows how much you know! They're models is what they are. They got nothing to do with whores. What they are most of them is college students, and when they can't pay for their schooling they let them take pictures of them, then they got the money for another year of school.

MARTHA: And how much do they get to be photographed that way?

OTTO: A thousand, maybe more.

MARTHA: I wouldn't do it, not even for a thousand.

OTTO: Nobody'd want to take your picture that way. Take a look what you look like.

MARTHA: That one there isn't pretty either.

OTTO: There's a difference.

MARTHA: Get me fixed up like that and give me a wig like hers, you'd never know me.

OTTO: I bet I'd know you anywhere.

MARTHA: Anyway, I don't need to, because I'm not in their situation.

Otto laughs.

You want me to read you what I just wrote?

OTTO: Some junk.

MARTHA: 'Cause I wrote it for you. Put your magazine away, then I'll read it to you.

OTTO: Jealous of a magazine, that's what you are. You don't got to be. Won't catch me jerking off.

MARTHA: Why's that?

OTTO: 'Cause a guy like me don't need to.

MARTHA *(Clears her throat)*: January 10th: Otto came to dinner here the first time. We had cold cuts and caviar. But Otto complained right away that it wasn't Russian but only regular.

OTTO: Got that right.

MARTHA: Wait, there's more! . . . I had no idea my Otto was such a gourmet. Now we're going to spend a nice evening together. *(She laughs)*

OTTO: Hanging onto every little thing. *(Short pause)* Junk like that.

MARTHA: Tomorrow early I'll write down everything else we do tonight. Just notes, but I can read them.

OTTO: Why'n'cha come on over here now and stop talking.

MARTHA *(Laughs)*: If that's what you want.

OTTO: Get undressed.

MARTHA: You too.

OTTO: A man don't have to get undressed all the time, a woman's different.

The dog's howling is closer and louder now.

Now the dog wants in.

MARTHA: Well, he can't. *(She gets undressed)*

OTTO: Just what I expected, now he starts in. Where's the leash?

MARTHA: Where it belongs.

OTTO: Son of a bitch!

MARTHA: On the chest there.

Otto takes the leash and goes out. The dog howls furiously. Otto whips him. Martha continues to herself.

The dog is part of me, but you can beat on him if you want to. Anyway he barks at people all the time so bad the neighbors complain about the noise, he deserves a beating.

OTTO *(Outside)*: Son of a bitch, be quiet.

The dog growls threateningly.

MARTHA *(To herself)*: He's not used to being outside so long by himself, he's impatient.

OTTO *(On the defensive; the dog is furious)*: Bastard, get off!

We hear the dog attacking. Otto yells.

MARTHA *(To herself, softly, almost laughing)*: He doesn't like being whipped, he's defending himself.

OTTO *(Outside, in the midst of battle)*: Son of a bitch, God damn. Down I said, get the hell off. *(Shouts)* Martha! The bastard's trying to bite me!

MARTHA *(Runs to Otto, calling)*: Down, Ralphie! Down! Get into your box! Go on, or you want Mommie to get angry with you?

Otto snorts.

And no more howling or Mommie'll give you something to howl about, you'll see!

The dog yaps cheerfully and trots off. Both Otto and Martha come back in.

OTTO: Came at me and tried to bite me, the bastard!

MARTHA: When someone hits him he defends himself. And he notices right away if someone's afraid of him or not. *(Laughs)*

OTTO: I'm not afraid of him. Next time I'll smash his head in. *(Pause)* That dog is a cunt-hound, that's what he is. I seen him sticking his head up your skirt.

Martha laughs.

You really must have had to look around to find a dog like that.

MARTHA: I'm freezing.

OTTO: Come on then.

They both lie down on the sofa. Pause.

MARTHA: What's the matter?

OTTO: Nothing. That dog's got to go.

January 11th: But it didn't turn out nice after all, and it was Ralphie's fault, because he called Otto's bluff. Now Otto is ready to kill Ralphie and me too. He wants revenge and keeps saying that Ralphie's got to go. But you don't have to worry, Ralphie, you can count on your mommie. He's got another think coming if he thinks I'd do that, that's going way too far.

January 15th: My Otto comes here every day now. But he really is a pig sometimes, I have to admit it, and I don't know why he acts that way. Being jealous of Ralphie is really dumb, but maybe that's normal for a man. But he won't discuss anything else anymore and won't let me talk him out of it and works himself up and gets rude, it gets on my nerves and wears me down. It's too bad because I really like Otto a lot and would do anything for him. It's really cold now and yesterday I got so annoyed with Otto I went home and forgot to fill up the oil heater for the night, so this morning it was so cold in the store I thought sure the pipes would be frozen. But thank God nothing happened! Sometimes I think Otto just imagines things. Hopefully he won't go on like that. Knock wood!

SCENE TWO

In the shop. Otto is lying on the sofa in the back room, smoking. Martha is working. They converse between rooms in loud voices.

MARTHA: A butcher shop is the kind of business you can depend on.

OTTO: Meat, everywhere you look.

MARTHA: You just have to get to know what everything is.

OTTO: Not interested.

MARTHA: If you knew something about it you could work here. I could certainly use some help.

OTTO: You think I'm gonna sit inside someplace all day selling dog food?

MARTHA: I could buy you a pickup and let you do the buying. A couple hours at the slaughterhouse in the morning and you could lay around the rest of the day. When you go to the market early yourself you can decide better what you want and what you don't, 'stead of just getting delivered like I do. But you got to know what you're doing. The buying's what can make or break you.

OTTO: What're you paying?

MARTHA: We'd just share everything together.

OTTO: I earn more the way I am.

MARTHA: How much?

OTTO: Fourteen hundred minimum.

MARTHA: Before or after taxes?

OTTO: After.

MARTHA: I do better than that.

OTTO: How much?

MARTHA: Two thousand in the summertime. In the winter I can get up to three thousand and better. *(Laughs)*

OTTO: Liar.

MARTHA: Why should I lie? You can look it up in last year's books.

OTTO: What do I care about your books?

MARTHA: On top of that I'm my own boss, and you're not.

OTTO: Who needs independence, it don't buy you a beer.

MARTHA: You never been your own boss, if you were you'd talk different.

OTTO: Nobody tells me what to do at work.

MARTHA: Never said they did.

OTTO: And when production's high we get a bonus. Sixty-five marks last month!

MARTHA: I wouldn't get into a sweat over any sixty-five marks.

OTTO: Because you storekeepers, you got no sense of proportion. Counting every penny.

MARTHA: Sure, because every penny's *mine*!

OTTO: Well, what about me? On the packing machines they keep count of every single thing you do.

MARTHA: I guess I just like my shop better.

OTTO: Disgusting. Somebody making that much just selling dog food, there ought to be a law.

MARTHA *(Laughs)*: Will you stop it? It's not just dog food, it's all the utility meats. I had to take the same courses and the same exams a regular butcher does, just like the men!

OTTO: Exactly.

MARTHA: My parents were butchers just like me, I grew up in the business. My father even used to supply a circus.

OTTO: Oh, tigers now, impressive.

MARTHA: But now that all the little circuses are gone, there's no business there. The Sarrasani Brothers wouldn't be interested. *(Laughs)* They got to think in quantity.

OTTO: Not a steak in the house for Chrissake.

MARTHA: Steak isn't a utility meat, silly.

OTTO: What I'm saying, you're no real butcher and this is no real butcher shop.

MARTHA: Of course it is. It's just we specialize. My father did the same, because he saw the way things were going. I could turn this place into a regular butcher shop any time I want, I got everything I need. But there's lots of regular butcher shops, and places like this are dying out; as long as there's just one around you can really do well.

OTTO: But a woman butcher, that's not normal, say what you like.

MARTHA: There's nothing not normal about it, it's just damn hard for a woman, that's all, but I did it!

OTTO: I'm glad I'm a man. No contest.

MARTHA: Well it'd be a lot easier if I was a man, I'll tell you that. But it's solid, just like my parents said. Sales are better all the time, the remodeling bills are almost paid off, and my house . . .

OTTO: . . . is bought and paid for with no rent to worry about!

MARTHA: That's a lie! The house is a third paid for and the rest is a mortgage which isn't too bad and less than paying rent, only I'm paying the rent to myself and not somebody else! *(She sniffs loudly, really worked up)*

OTTO: Listen to her talk, nothing feminine about her!

MARTHA: I say what I think, that's all.

OTTO: But a woman's got to be female. Sometimes you got to look to be sure.

MARTHA: What?

OTTO: Don't look at me like that, I read it on the sports page, where they got these Russians who dress

themselves up like women so they can win gold medals.
Lift up the old apron there and let's have a sex check.

MARTHA: You're really disgusting sometimes.

OTTO *(Laughs)*: And 'cause you couldn't never find yourself
a man before I come along and took pity on you, you
gotta admit it looks suspicious.

MARTHA: I had plenty opportunities, let me tell you,
working at a counter all day long. But I don't throw
myself away on anyone.

OTTO: So how'd you lose your virginity? Do it to yourself in
the middle of the night, without the blessings of the
church?

MARTHA: Oh, stop it. It's so long ago I can't even remember
now.

OTTO: I'm not surprised, at your age.

MARTHA: Fine. *(Pause)* When you're in the shop from
morning to night trying to make ends meet there's not a
lot of room for private life.

OTTO: Surrounded by a lot of dead animals all the time, that
can't be good for your state of mind.

MARTHA: I don't let anybody talk to me about my shop. I
got a right to be proud of it. Everybody says so. A
woman alone has it hard.

OTTO: You got a dog.

MARTHA: We always had a dog.

OTTO: He don't like me one little bit, that dog of yours.
(Laughs) Because I'm here.

MARTHA: Naturally, he's not used to you.

OTTO: He'd like to tear my throat out, your dog would.

MARTHA: He's not going to hurt you.

OTTO: You think I'm afraid of him?

Martha says nothing.

He's so fat he couldn't hurt anybody anyway.

MARTHA: They use their weight when they attack.

OTTO: Then I guess I'd have to shoot him.

MARTHA: If you had a gun.

OTTO: I already got one.

MARTHA: Where?

OTTO: Back home, where it belongs.

MARTHA: You got all kinds of things.

OTTO: Small-caliber, but with power to penetrate.

MARTHA: At the slaughterhouse they got a gun big enough
to kill an elephant.

OTTO: I don't need to kill no elephant.

MARTHA: What if one attacked you?

OTTO: There aren't any elephants around here.

MARTHA: If one broke out of the circus then there would be.

OTTO: All you can think about is animals, nothing else.

MARTHA: I got an imagination, that's all.

OTTO: What it is is being alone too much, imagination's got
nothing to do with it.

MARTHA: Now I got you.

February 5th: Since I've been around Otto so much I've started
looking around when I'm on the street if anybody's looking at me.
I don't have any big effect, but they don't ignore me either.
Parenthesis: men, exclamation point, close parenthesis. *(She
chuckles to herself)* I'd like Otto so much more if he just wasn't so
ungrateful. A woman gives up a lot when she doesn't pay any
attention to love, the way I was. I know that now. Why was that?
Anyway, I know that I'm grateful to Otto just for coming into my
life. If he wants to he can stay. He practically lives at my place
already. But when he's been there for a while he always starts in
again about Ralphie and says the most awful things. Then he

starts in on what I did before I met him. Sometimes I feel like telling him I masturbated myself, just so he'd stop talking about Ralphie, but I don't have the nerve. Time will tell! This weekend we went to the zoo. My idea, because it's been years since I went to the zoo and at home we just argue all the time. Anyway, it was cold as ice and Otto got a terrible chill because he just wore his suit jacket although I told and told him. It's going to freeze again tonight, the radio says, as low as ten degrees. Really winter. Quotation marks: white nights, quotation marks. I'm not sleeping well just now. Funny, an old cow like me *(Smiles to herself)* thinking all the the time about my Otto. The last few days he hasn't been here every night. Where is he? Is there still a chance for love when you're forty, question mark. He's not here again tonight, my Otto leaves me alone. I'm listening to "Request Concert" with Fred Rausch. Beautiful exclamation point.

SCENE THREE

Martha and Otto making love.

OTTO: If you're gonna mess around with a dog, you won't get any loving from me.
MARTHA: That's a lie and you know it.
OTTO: So you say.
MARTHA: I ought to know.
OTTO: The way he stuck his nose up under your dress when you turned around, I noticed that the first time he did it.
MARTHA: Every dog does that.
OTTO: He does it 'cause he wants something.
MARTHA: And what do you think that is?
OTTO: Shut up!

MARTHA: Ow, now you're hurting me.

OTTO (*Snorting*): 'Cause I was coming. The last time you're
    getting it from me though.

MARTHA: Easy enough to say afterwards.

OTTO: When I say something I stick to it.

Pause.

MARTHA: I just can't figure you out.

OTTO: You can't figure men out is what it is.

MARTHA: I'm learning.

OTTO: It's something you can't learn, you got it or you don't.

MARTHA: I can't do anything right far as you're concerned,
    can I?

OTTO: It's for your own good. Otherwise I wouldn't take the
    trouble. But as long as that dog's around it's no good.

MARTHA: What?

OTTO: He takes your mind off me.

MARTHA: He does no such thing!

OTTO: Still pretending, when it's high time you owned up
    the truth! I seen through what you're up to. You think
    I'm blind? The way he's always sneaking around you and
    sticking his nose in where he's got no business to. And
    the way he hates me.

MARTHA: It's because you're afraid of him.

OTTO: Excuses is all that is.

MARTHA: I'm getting up now.

OTTO: Sure, why not, it's all over.

Martha gets up, gets dressed.

I seen through it.

MARTHA: What a pig you are.

OTTO: A hint is all I need.

MARTHA: There's nothing to hint at.

OTTO: Then let's drop the subject, since it's all settled. *(He turns onto his side)* Wake me up in half an hour.

MARTHA: Going to take a little nap?

OTTO: Half an hour, I'm tired.

MARTHA: Then I might as well re-pot the rubber tree now.

OTTO: As long as you're quiet.

MARTHA: Naturally.

Short pause.

OTTO: You got a way with flowers, I'll give you that.

MARTHA: Because I got a secret. *(Laughs)* The dirt I use, I get it from the field back of the church. It's better than any potting soil.

OTTO: Stealing.

MARTHA: You go back there and look real careful, you'll see little holes all over the place. That's me.

OTTO: It's still stealing.

MARTHA: A little dirt? Who's going to care?

Pause.

OTTO: You're not normal, you're nothing to look at and live all alone.

MARTHA: We can't all be as much in demand as you are.

OTTO: Nothing to look at at all. A woman ought to look like it's a pleasure to look at her.

MARTHA: I never claimed to be good-looking.

OTTO: It's a good thing you don't.

MARTHA: So what're you doing here? If I may be allowed to ask.

OTTO: I feel sorry for you.

MARTHA: I don't need your sympathy, it won't pay the rent. *(Pause)* Come up to the apartment with me tonight and stay over like a sensible person.

OTTO: Nope.

MARTHA: Why not?

OTTO: None of your business.

MARTHA: It is so.

OTTO: You keep on like this and you're gonna lose me entirely.

MARTHA: Are you seeing someone else?

OTTO: A man has always got more than one iron in the fire.

MARTHA: I see.

OTTO: Let me get some sleep now. Wake me at . . . ten after seven.

MARTHA: All right.

February 16th: Otto, where are you. Parenthesis: desire. Close parenthesis.

February 22nd: I often think that the doorbell is going to ring and it's going to be Otto at the door. I wonder if he'll come back? I keep the diary going, even though there's not much to put into it these days. Business is very good. I took in eight hundred and sixty-seven sixty-three today. Hopefully Otto will come back. When you're not so young anymore it's hard to find someone that suits you. I think he will come back. I have a little cold and I'm taking some pills for it. They're called Pyramidon and they're not bad. Ralphie is a nuisance. He likes being the only one again. *(Laughs)* The little bastard. Otto, I love you. Come back, exclamation point and period.

SCENE FOUR

In the shop.

OTTO: So how you been?

MARTHA *(Laughs)*: You're back again.

OTTO: Just dropped by, see how you're doing.

MARTHA: Fine.

OTTO: Me too.

MARTHA: You looked better before you left.

OTTO: That's life.

MARTHA: Some life, from the looks of it!

OTTO: I need my freedom.

MARTHA: Well, you got it.

OTTO: Don't believe anything I say, do you?

MARTHA: I've got eyes in my head, don't I? *(Pause)* Well don't just stand there like a customer waiting for a pound of liver, come around back.

OTTO: OK.

They go into the back room.

Still got the ashtray you got special for me right out on the table, you start smoking or what?

MARTHA: Sure. Wild man.

OTTO: Getting big ideas because I come back, I can see that already.

MARTHA: I'm just happy, that's all. You go away all fat and sassy and come back looking like you been run over by a truck . . .

OTTO: I was on the road three days.

MARTHA: Throwing your money away.

OTTO: My money.

MARTHA: Just the same.

OTTO: The first couple days I stayed inside the whole time, just watched TV and stuff. And then I couldn't take it anymore and I just took off. Three days and nights, on the town, like they say. *(Laughs)*

Pause.

MARTHA: And I thought all along you had another girl. *(Short pause)* Now you're back I can see I'll have to take care of you right. That's how it ought to be, anyway; a man's got to raise some hell sometimes. It doesn't matter. If you need some money I can loan you some.

OTTO: I don't borrow off women.

MARTHA: OK, don't, then.

OTTO: I'm beat.

MARTHA: Go on upstairs to the apartment, give yourself a good scrubbing, get something out of the fridge to settle your stomach, there's plenty there, and then lie down and get some sleep. And in the morning you can go back in to work.

OTTO: Right.

MARTHA: You had your fun, you lived a little, fine. Now everything's back to normal.

OTTO: You coming up with me?

MARTHA: I can't lock up at eleven in the morning just because you happen to blow in the door. Lunchtime I'll come up and make us some pancakes and back bacon. I'll wake you.

OTTO: Don't even want me.

MARTHA: One thing at a time. Take a look at yourself in the mirror, like a bum. Make yourself presentable, then we'll see.

OTTO: Stuff you say.

MARTHA: It looks like you got your nose broken.

OTTO: It was a sneaky punch. *(Laughs)*
MARTHA: I see.

Otto laughs again.

Anybody else sneak up on you?
OTTO: No whores, if that's what you mean.
MARTHA: Look me in the eye.
OTTO: No whores . . . only sixty-year-old ones, anyway.
MARTHA: That I can believe.

Pause.

OTTO: I'll come back if you like, Martha.
MARTHA: What else? There's the key; but for goodness' sake
wash and get undressed before you get into bed, and
don't drink any more in your condition, or you'll wet
your pants like you did that other time.
OTTO: You bitch.
MARTHA: I know you.
OTTO *(Going)*: Bitch.

Martha laughs.

February 25th: Otto is back again. At last.

SCENE FIVE

Martha and Otto in the apartment.

MARTHA: In a couple days carnival will be over and we won't
have been to one thing.
OTTO: Who needs it?
MARTHA: You got to give everything a try, otherwise what
would there be to talk about?

OTTO: So how much'd the tickets cost?

MARTHA: That's my secret, 'cause I invited you.

OTTO *(Reads)*: "A Night in the Tropics." Not cheap, anyhow.

MARTHA: It don't matter.

OTTO: One of these here balls can cost a fortune, that's what I heard.

MARTHA: Well, we'll find out. It's my treat.

OTTO: We decide to go, I'll pay. That's the man's job.

MARTHA: If you want to.

OTTO: I pay or I don't go.

MARTHA: Much obliged! . . . Might as well enjoy ourselves while we're able. *(She pokes around in some shopping bags)*

OTTO: What you got there?

MARTHA: See for yourself!

OTTO: A costume?

MARTHA: Of course, it's no fun otherwise.

OTTO: If you think I'm putting on a mask you got another think coming. I'd look like a sissy.

MARTHA: Can't know unless you try.

OTTO: So what's it supposed to be?

MARTHA: Guess.

She giggles to herself and puts on the costume. Pause. Otto has to laugh too.

It's a flower-girl. You can tell right away, look: Eliza Doolittle. *My Fair Lady*!

Laughs. Otto laughs in agreement. Martha hums, sketches a few dance steps.

"I could have danced all night . . ."

OTTO *(Interrupting)*: So who'm I supposed to be?

MARTHA: Professor Higgins, who else?

OTTO: Who's he?

MARTHA: Honestly, don't you ever go to the movies? He's a high-class English gentleman.

Otto laughs.

I thought about it a long time before I got the idea. Here, all you have to do is put it on, it's all there.

OTTO: You're out of your mind, what did all this cost?

MARTHA: Rented.

OTTO: Where from?

MARTHA: They have places where that's all you do is rent carnival costumes. *(Short pause)* Didn't know your old lady was so smart, did you?

OTTO: You know, I never been to one of these big affairs in my whole life?

MARTHA: I have, but it was years and years ago. You have to start sometime. Stick with me.

OTTO: You know I'm actually a little scared?

MARTHA: What of? *(She starts singing again)*

March 1st: It was nice. Although there weren't enough people there to really make it seem like a real party. If I'd known that before I would have got tickets to a different ball. It's not important. Otto can't dance, that's why he didn't want to go, I realize that now. I danced with other people and he got really mad. I asked him why he didn't tell me in the first place, how was I supposed to know, and then he said he forgot how. *(Laughs)* I still could, even though it's been years. And even if I hadn't been able to, I could have let myself be hauled around like plenty of other women there. Otto got awfully drunk.

April 12th: Tomorrow is Otto's birthday. Aries, the Ram. *(Laughs)* And I'm a Leo. *(Laughs)* Thirty-eight, he says, question mark. I finally thought of a nice surprise for Otto, colon: a fancy modern quartz watch with a real gold band, exclamation point. It's the last word, no numbers on it at all, completely modern, just a button where you push and it gives you hours, minutes, seconds, day and month. *(Laughs)* That will make him sit up and take notice. Price: a hundred sixty-eight ninety-five, and ninety-three ninety for the band. From the jewelry counter in the department store. I looked in a couple of shop windows on my way home, they're much more expensive other places. Dash, exclamation point. What will Otto think, question mark.

April 14th: The watch wasn't a big success. I was looking at him when he opened it and I'm certain it was a surprise, parenthesis I have eyes close parenthesis, but he just said it was fancy sissy stuff and he liked his old one better, which is really cheap-looking and ugly. *(Pause)* I told him that the store would exchange it for another one or give him a gift certificate for the amount it cost. Then he at least looked at it. Parenthesis Otto has no idea what things cost close parenthesis. At first he left it lying around, but later he picked it up and started fiddling with it, and I thought, aha! *(Laughs)* We'll see now whether he wants it or not. If he wears it, fine, and if he doesn't, I don't care, parenthesis even though it cost good money and isn't some piece of junk, close parenthesis.

April 19th: We can't go on like this forever. I told Otto but he won't believe me. He has to be the boss about everything, and I just won't have it. I'm somebody too. I tell him and tell him but he pays no attention. I like Otto a lot but he's going to have to stop thinking he can walk all over me whenever he's in a bad mood instead of acting like a decent person, colon: like helping out with the shop for example. Business this month is very good three exclamation points. When I total up in the evening Otto looks over my shoulder and gets so mad he can't see straight. Yesterday night nine hundred forty-five twenty-three, barely fifty off a thousand-mark day. And instead of being pleased he gets so mad he nearly chokes, the idiot. Because he's envious. Otherwise we're doing all right.

SCENE SIX

In the shop. Martha working, Otto in the back room. They have to speak loudly. The radio is playing folk music.

OTTO: 'S'r'any beer left?

MARTHA: Still drinking? *(Pause)* If you drunk five already, there's none left.

OTTO: Four, can't you count?

MARTHA: Then one must still be in the shopping bag, 'cause I bought five.

OTTO *(Checks)*: That was it.

Pause.

MARTHA: You coming upstairs with me when I'm finished here?

OTTO: Don't expect me stay here every night.

MARTHA: Going on another one of your little outings?

OTTO: Something going on, anyhow.

MARTHA: And what would that be?

OTTO: None of your business.

MARTHA: Got a new "friend"? *(She emphasizes the "friend")*

OTTO: A good one, right.

MARTHA *(Coming into the back room)*: I see.

OTTO: The way I took pity on you, the least you can do is leave me alone and be quiet.

MARTHA: You told me you were going to stop all your
    running around.
OTTO: I gotta have my freedom, nobody been able to lock
    me up yet. *(Pause)* You can't get enough, can you?
MARTHA: If you say so.

Pause.

OTTO: Wanting it that much ain't normal, you know.
MARTHA: I thought it was natural when you love somebody.
OTTO: Well, not tonight. Somebody else's turn. *(Long pause)*
    Everything in its place. You ought to be glad you got a
    man at all, not everybody can say that.
MARTHA: I'm not ungrateful. I give you everything I have.
OTTO: Big deal.
MARTHA: It's not all that cheap keeping you satisfied.
OTTO: You want me to go? Just say the word, any time.
MARTHA: And come crawling back again, too.
OTTO: Cunt.
MARTHA: I'm just stating a fact.
OTTO: So who paid for the Tropical Ball, you or me?
MARTHA: I had a wonderful time. I said thank you.
OTTO: A hundred and sixty-three marks altogether!
MARTHA: Yes.

Pause.

OTTO: There's no point us having a discussion like this. I
    don't need no woman coming on to me like that.
MARTHA: I'm not doing anything to you. I love you.
OTTO: You know a lot about love, you do.
MARTHA: But I'm a businesswoman, you can't just push me
    around like a little kid. My independence counts for
    something too.
OTTO: Will you knock it off with your fucking

independence? You think I don't know what a fine
upstanding citizen you are and what an asshole I am?

MARTHA: I never said that.

OTTO: But that's what you think.

Pause.

MARTHA: Come home with me when I finish up, be sensible!

OTTO: Jesus you're pigheaded.

MARTHA: All right then, I'm pigheaded. *(Short pause)* I
bought some veal steaks, they won't keep.

OTTO: You got a refrigerator.

MARTHA: They won't keep long in the fridge either.

OTTO *(After a pause)*: You want it, you can have it here. I'm
not coming with you, I told you I got something else on.

MARTHA: You don't have anything planned.

OTTO: Little bird tell you that? Come on, here or nowhere.

MARTHA: Well, here then, since you won't be reasonable.

OTTO: You never know, it might be a long time until the
next one.

MARTHA: Yes.

OTTO: Come on, get over here, don't waste time. Just get rid
of the underpants, that's good enough. *(Pause)* What's
up?

MARTHA: Nothing. I don't want to after all, I thought it
over. Go along now, then you won't come home so late.
You'll have to excuse me for disturbing your relaxation,
but I'm finished and I want to lock up.

OTTO: You're not finished yet.

MARTHA: I'll take care of the rest in the morning. And you
don't want to waste any time.

OTTO: OK. *(He gets up and goes)* You thought over what
you're doing?

MARTHA: That's right. See you.

OTTO: Maybe. *(Exit)*

MARTHA *(After a pause, to herself)*: You were right.

April 30th: Otto has been gone eight days again. I saw it coming, but what could I do? I'm not as upset as I expected to be, after all this is the second time. All I really have to do is decide what I'm going to say to him when he comes back again like last time. I wonder if he really has another girlfriend? When I try to imagine it it hurts me, but I'd still like to know what kind of woman she is. Maybe I should spy on him, follow him after work. *(Laughs)* If he really does have somebody else, it would spoil everything. The dream would be over, because she must be a real idiot if she puts up with more nonsense from him than I do. Maybe he only says he's got someone to make me jealous, though. Or just some old witch exclamation point. I won't feel jealous until I see what sort of competition she is and whether she's at least prettier than me. If she isn't even better looking he must not have any eyes in his head at all. Business is off parenthesis summery weather close parenthesis. Four hundred eighty-seven sixty in the cash register today.

SCENE SEVEN

In the living quarters. Water is running in the bathtub.

OTTO *(Loud)*: Put some clean underwear out where I can get at it.

MARTHA *(From outside)*: What?

OTTO: I said bring me some clean underwear, you got your head up your ass or what?

MARTHA *(Calling out)*: Right away. *(Pause. She enters)* I'll put them on the radiator for you so they don't get damp.

OTTO: OK.

MARTHA: You want me to scrub your back for you?

OTTO: Don't need it.

MARTHA: When a person got something they don't know what it's worth. Here you got a bathroom and a place to stay and someone to wash your back for you. And where do you go off to?

OTTO: Wouldn't you like to know.

MARTHA: I can imagine.

OTTO: Imagine what you like. *(Makes a smacking sound with his lips)*

MARTHA: Spare me the details.

OTTO: What're you looking at?

MARTHA: Nothing.

OTTO: Like what you see?

MARTHA *(Laughs)*: You idiot.

OTTO: I used to have a good build. You should of seen me. I used to work out.

MARTHA: It wouldn't do you any harm now, instead of your other activities.

OTTO: No flab, anywhere you look.

MARTHA: What about there?

OTTO: Where?

MARTHA *(Formal)*: On your ab-*do*-men.

OTTO: That's all muscle, whadda you know about it?

MARTHA: You want me to scrub your back for you?

OTTO: Like she's never seen a man before.

Martha laughs.

OK, but gently!

Martha washes his back.

In China they got these bathhouses. When they give you

a bath in those places they really get to you. Because
they got sensitivity, those geishas.

MARTHA: I'm no geisha. It's important to get your back
clean, that's all. *(Pause)* There. Don't be long now,
dinner's waiting.

OTTO: What're we having?

MARTHA: Let it be a surprise.

SCENE EIGHT

In the bedroom, nighttime.

OTTO: What I'd do is lease the shop to someone and then
just take it easy.

MARTHA: We couldn't live on that.

OTTO: Well, I could get a half-time job somewheres.

MARTHA: Give up my business and fiddle my time away! I'd
have to be out of my mind.

OTTO: The stuff you say. Nothing feminine about you.

MARTHA: Just because I got a brain.

OTTO: But no female charm. *(Pause)* And what kind of man
is it is got to say "The little woman? Oh, she's a
independent butcher who makes more than I do?"

MARTHA: You ought to be glad.

Pause.

OTTO: I don't feel right when I'm around you. I told the
guys at work about it and they all say I'm right. *(Short
pause)* If you was at least good-looking.

MARTHA: If I *was* good-looking I certainly wouldn't be as
independent as I am.

OTTO: Least there'd be an excuse.

MARTHA: Don't be silly. You have an inferiority complex, that's what's wrong with you.

OTTO: I got no time to have no inferiority complexes.

Pause.

MARTHA: Well, you heard my offer. Come work here. I'll give you eight hundred fifty a month and no rent or board to pay. And when I can afford it you'll get more.

OTTO: I'd go nuts in no time.

MARTHA: That's only because the idea of a woman boss doesn't suit you.

OTTO: Well, it ain't normal, everybody says so.

MARTHA: I don't have any way of knowing whether it is or not. I just know I love my job.

OTTO: That's not normal either.

MARTHA: If you worked for me you wouldn't talk like that long. Think about it anyway, my offer. Eight hundred fifty cash and no expenses.

OTTO: No way. Man of my word.

May 26th: Otto is moody. Maybe he has a complex because I'm not good-looking. But he's not so good-looking either. But I don't tell him, because he thinks he's really something. Otherwise I'm doing fine and so is Otto. He really lives here now. Exclamation point. Maybe that's why we fight so much. He always has to have the last word, but I'm right most of the time. Because he always says just the opposite of what I say, no matter what. He always has to be the smart one and show he's better than me. Maybe once he's knocked me down far enough he'll pick me up again? Maybe a person ought to just close their eyes to it because he needs it as a man. Resolution colon be more diplomatic exclamation point. A lot of times I'd like to talk to someone and I realize I don't have one really good woman friend. I'll have to make some. Business is bad. Much too hot. Yesterday we went to the Löwenbräukeller and sat outside in the garden. It was nice. Otto was in a good mood. He didn't get drunk at all. I love him a lot. Does he love me too question mark.

SCENE NINE

In the shop. Back room.

MARTHA: In broad daylight, what if anyone saw?

OTTO: No one's gonna see.

MARTHA: I wouldn't dare, it's Saturday morning, there's customers coming in all the time.

OTTO: You're just chicken.

MARTHA: Well what if someone did come in?

OTTO: We can straighten up before they see anything. I done this plenty of times, I'll have him tucked away again before anyone could notice.

MARTHA: It's no use, I just can't.

OTTO: Suppose they did see. Good for them. Let 'em see you don't give a damn what they think when it comes to the man in your life.

MARTHA: You'd like it if my customers found out and started avoiding me like the plague. This neighborhood's so damn Catholic they got no pity at all.

OTTO: What do you need a man for, you're already married to this butcher shop.

MARTHA: I do enough for you already.

OTTO : A little humility, that's what you need.

MARTHA: Crap.

Pause.

OTTO: Ok, then come on over and give me a hum job.

MARTHA: What's that?

OTTO: Something a woman can do who wants to give her man a thrill. You don't got to get undressed or anything, there's nothing for anyone to see. Only me.

MARTHA: But what am I supposed to do?

OTTO: Gimme a blow job, you never heard of it?

MARTHA: I never did that in my life.

OTTO: First time for everything.

Pause.

MARTHA: All you care about is getting your own way.

OTTO: Right. Unzip my fly and . . . easy! You bite me and I'll knock you sideways.

MARTHA: I wouldn't do that.

OTTO: Here, I'll sit down and you can kneel between my legs.

MARTHA: All right.

OTTO: And when I come, swallow it, all right? No spitting it out.

MARTHA: And what if I can't swallow it, what if I have to spit?

OTTO: You can try for once. Like a real woman would.

MARTHA: Yes.

June 9th: We live on my money. Parenthesis except for the Tropical Ball close parenthesis. That's not right. I have more to spend, even if he hates to admit it, but just the same. He has to be his own boss. I don't know if he's given up his room at the boarding house or not. He's always around anyway. He says he hasn't given it up, but he lies sometimes too. He always has to be showing me that he's a man and I'm not. I haven't been able to get him over that so far. I have to be even more diplomatic. But I don't know where I'm going to get the patience. Everybody has his faults, and Otto's not so bad really. He is dumb, though. When he has me down and can walk all over me, that doesn't mean he's really on top exclamation point. I'm no conquest to be proud of. But he needs it. He's really pushing me now. But I'll go along with him as far as I can. Now there's things I can't even put in my diary dot dot dot. What will the future bring question mark.

SCENE TEN

In the living room. TV on, perhaps a sports show.

MARTHA: People have to pull together, Otto, otherwise you never accomplish anything in this world. *(Pause)* Do you understand? *(Pause)* You just work against me.

OTTO: I'm watching TV, do you mind?

MARTHA: You eat and sleep here.

OTTO: I still got my room.

MARTHA: Then give it up.

OTTO: That'd suit you just fine.

MARTHA: There's a lot of things a woman's got to know about love, I realize that now. But a person has got to watch out or you just sink without a trace before you know it.

OTTO: You had to learn who the man was.

MARTHA: Back at the beginning, remember, I told you you could read everything I wrote in my diary? But you never did.

OTTO: Boring.

MARTHA: And I haven't offered to let you read it for a long time. Here it is.

OTTO: A diary's supposed to be secret.

MARTHA: Maybe.

OTTO: I don't want to butt in, it's none of my business.

MARTHA: But I wrote something in it just now just for you.

OTTO: You giving me my two weeks' notice? *(Laughs)*

MARTHA: Don't be silly. A poem. The first poem I've written since I can't remember when. Because I've been thinking about us. You want me to read it to you?

OTTO: Do what you like.

MARTHA: I'd like to read it out loud. Turn the TV down.

OTTO: Not while the sports is on.

MARTHA: It's my TV, Otto.

OTTO: Right. *(He stands up and turns the TV off)* I'm listening.

MARTHA *(Laughs)*: I don't even have a title yet: "Night brought your shadow to my door. I stand and try to stretch but I am small. All the flowers flower fast, the ones outside as well. I long to be your wife in word and deed. Stand by me when I am weary, I will stand by you the same. And do not step where I have planted seeds for both of us. Be careful." *(Pause)* That's all.

OTTO: What kind of poem is it when it doesn't even rhyme?

MARTHA: Just the same, you couldn't have written it down like I did.

OTTO: Nope.

June 12th: It was no use, no matter how hard I worked on it. He's right: a poem has to rhyme. He says he doesn't feel right when he's around me, and it's my fault. Because a woman butcher isn't normal. Maybe he's right, but what good does that do? You have to make the best of things the way they are. Parenthesis six hundred twenty-two eleven in the till today, it's hotter than blazes exclamation point close parenthesis. I'm going on a diet for him. Maybe then he'd forget about the butcher business. I weigh a hundred forty-one pounds now. I want to get down to a hundred thirty. I have to watch out though, a hard worker needs his health. But you have to give something up for love. I start on the 15th: a strict diet. I look in the mirror a lot these days. *(Laughs)* I realize I'm no sex-bomb, but I'm female enough. *(Laughs)* But Otto's never satisfied. He can be nice, though. When he's a little drunk, just a little, that's when he's nicest. Those are wonderful times. I try to influence him but suddenly he notices and he closes right up and then it's bad. When he's totally sober he's rude all the time because of his being not so well off as me. What a lot of nonsense. Everything else is fine. Maybe we should take a vacation together question mark. In parenthesis but what about the store question mark, close parenthesis.

SCENE ELEVEN

The living room. Martha under a sunlamp.

MARTHA: You'll see, it gives you a wonderful tan.

OTTO: And in the meantime I go blind. *(Pause)* While you got your eyes closed and can't see anything like you are now I could sneak away and you'd never see me again.

MARTHA: You'd be back soon enough.

OTTO: Right. *(Pause)* "The use of this sunlamp without the appropriate protective sunglasses is forbidden."

MARTHA: But if I use them I'll be white around the eyes and everybody'll know it wasn't real sun but only a sunlamp.

OTTO: This way it's bad for your eyes.

MARTHA: You really want me to put them on?

OTTO: On account of your eyes.

MARTHA: Well, if I have white rings around them later don't
get on me about it.

OTTO: No. Your eyes are what's important.

MARTHA: Are you worried about me?

OTTO: I just want to see the directions followed.

Martha laughs.

June 28th: Otto's off again. He'll come back soon enough. I'm not
going to worry. He'll be back in a few days. He only needs to see
how good he has it here.

July 10th: Not a sign of Otto. I'm worried. I wonder if I should
call up where he works and ask if he's there? I hope nothing has
happened to him. But I don't think so, because then he'd need me
and would have let me know already. I wonder if I'll ever see him
again question mark. I often think of times past exclamation
point. I wonder if I did something wrong. I think I must have, but
what. I know it wasn't wrong to try to keep him from beating me
down all the time. Maybe he imagined something, that's all it
could have been. I hope he's doing well. I'm fine. So is the shop.
Only Ralphie is making a pest of himself. I think a lot about taking
a vacation alone. Now's the best time exclamation point. And the
business can stand it, other people close for holidays and the
customers come back. But I'm stuck with the dumb dog. I wonder
where Otto is right now question mark.

August 4th: This photo shows Otto and me at the Tropical Ball.
Parenthesis in remembrance close parenthesis.

September 1st: All alone. Longing period.

The Nest

Martha
Kurt
Stefan

Act One

SCENE ONE

In the apartment, late in the evening. The TV is running. Martha is noticeably pregnant; she is knitting ties on piecework to earn some extra money. Kurt has nodded off.

TV ANNOUNCER *(Female)*: You've been watching the Heidelberg Municipal Theater production of *Upper Austria*: a play by the Bavarian author Franz Xaver Kroetz. Coming up next: the late edition of "The News Today."

Kurt has woken up.

MARTHA: Want to switch it off?

KURT: Might as well, we seen the news already.

Goes to switch off the set. Martha laughs.

What's so funny?

MARTHA: Don't you remember, that just happened in the show we were watching, exactly the same.

KURT: What did?

MARTHA: Only *you* went to sleep, the guy in the show
didn't.

KURT: Yeah, well let him put in as much overtime as I do
and not spend so much time shooting his mouth off,
then he'd know what it's like and maybe go to sleep too.

Pause.

MARTHA: No, it wasn't realistic.

KURT: Not at all, I could tell you that much.

MARTHA: But you got to admit you looked a little silly too
when I told you, "I caught, Kurtie!" You remember.

KURT: I was surprised is all.

Pause.

MARTHA: And I would have fought to have the baby anyway,
if you hadn't wanted it like the man in the show.

KURT: He didn't have any idea what he wanted, that guy. A
man has got to know what he wants, then everything's
OK. And somebody who's afraid of his own kid, that's
totally not normal.

MARTHA: Because he had inferiority complexes.

KURT: What for? I'm a truckdriver like him, you see me
having any?

MARTHA: No, that's true, we don't.

KURT: Sure.

MARTHA *(After a pause)*: And anyway there's no comparison
because you're a truckdriver and he was just a
deliveryman.

KURT: And that's right too, it's like they always say in
Drivers School, your Class II license entitles you to a
real job, not like your Class III. *(Pause)* Let's get to bed,
tomorrow's another day.

MARTHA *(Nods):* All right. *(Pause. She looks over the work she's done)* I'm not going to earn much at this rate.

KURT: Shouldn't be working at all now!

MARTHA: Practice makes perfect. *(Smiles)* But it doesn't amount to much yet. How long did the play last, anyway?

KURT: Good hour at least.

MARTHA: Three ties. *(Short pause)* That's not much.

KURT: One fifty.

MARTHA: I got to do better than that. You can do as many as ten an hour, that's what it says in the instructions, that would be five marks an hour, that's not so bad.

KURT: You'll get there.

MARTHA: That's right.

SCENE TWO

In the bedroom. Kurt is already in bed; Martha is getting ready for the night. Outside a squad car with blaring (European-style ooh-GAH! ooh-GAH!) siren rushes by. Pause.

KURT: It's nice, ain't it? When you hear 'em go tearing by like that, and you know there's no way they're coming here, because there's nothing wrong with us—no problem.

MARTHA: "A clear conscience is the softest pillow."

KURT: Exactly. *(Pause)* Are you glad you married me?

MARTHA: Why wouldn't I be? I got a hard-working man who's good to me . . .

KURT: You sure didn't feel that way to start with. You couldn't see me at all, you forgotten?

MARTHA: Always coming back to that again, sooner or later . . . !

KURT: Well, it's true.

MARTHA: When you're young you still got illusions, you can't blame a person for that.

KURT: But I wasn't an illusion, huh?

MARTHA: Thank God, no. . . . Illusions pass.

Short pause.

KURT: You were always my illusion.

MARTHA *(Smiles. Pause. She also lies down. . .)*: It's moving . . . you want to listen?

Kurt nods, lays head on her belly.

Hear anything? All over now. *(Smiles)* Every time you listen, he stops right away. And you should feel him kick all the rest of the time, the little stinker.

KURT: He can tell already it's his papa.

MARTHA: Um-hmm.

Pause.

KURT: Sometimes I still really want to.

MARTHA: You got to control yourself.

KURT: I guess. *(Pause)* But I read in the paper where you can do it right up to the day almost, I read it.

MARTHA: What kind of paper was that?

KURT: It was in the *Star*.

MARTHA: Naturally. Let's just do what the doctor says, not what the *Star* says, all right? Three months before, two months after.

KURT: I'm only talking . . .

Pause.

MARTHA: Go to sleep, why don't you?

KURT: OK. Good night.

SCENE THREE

In the apartment, Saturday afternoon.

KURT: Let's get started.

MARTHA: I was absolutely shocked.

KURT: I won't be.

MARTHA: You just wait. I got all the prices, down to the last penny.

KURT: Go ahead.

MARTHA: I figured Adele has experience, what with three kids already. And she's a friend.

KURT: Sure.

Pause.

MARTHA: OK, now, pay attention! *(She reads from a long list)* First: the baby carriage! The baby carriage's hard, 'cause you have to make decisions. You should have gone to look at them with us.

KURT: When did I have time?

MARTHA: What I'd like is one of the really modern ones, 'cause they've got advantages over the other models.

KURT: Like what?

MARTHA: You can open up the top part like windows so the baby can look out and the sun can get in and it's not all dark. It's supposed to be an important improvement for the baby.

KURT: Windows are always good.

MARTHA: But expensive: 279 marks they cost.

KURT *(Proudly)*: You got it.

MARTHA: If it's OK with you. . . . The mattress for it is 17.80, that's standard.

Kurt nods.

And a "Paidi-Bed" is absolutely basic, anybody with any self-respect has one.

KURT: "Paidi-Bed." *(Nods)* There's a word for you.

MARTHA: Really. Paidi-Bed, Varietta Model: 195 marks.

KURT: Expensive.

MARTHA: But really beautiful.

KURT *(Laughs)*: OK, you got it!

MARTHA: The mattress for it's 75, and the shield is 15 and a coverlet is 59.50, you have to have them.

KURT: You got 'em!

MARTHA: Adele can loan us the portable crib and the baby scales, that's a big savings.

KURT: We don't need to borrow anything.

MARTHA: Oh, don't be silly—everbody does it, because those are things you only need a couple months. People with good friends always borrow them, even when they *could* afford their own.

KURT: All right then.

MARTHA: Next: [listen to this: *(Reads)*] "Everything baby needs to wear to be snug as a bug in a rug!" *(Laughs)*

KURT: Let's have it!

MARTHA: First basic wardrobe of shirts, jackets, rompers and diapers, special offer for expectant mothers, already assembled: 235.70.

KURT: You got it.

MARTHA: Two small "Sleepysacks," 15.90 apiece is 31.80. I already bought booty pants, short pants and two sweaters, that was 54.60. And I have to get a large-size "Sleepysacks," that's 19.80.

KURT: I thought you had two already?

MARTHA: You need a big one too.

KURT: What for?

MARTHA: I'll explain everything, just let me get through it
all first.

KURT: Fine.

MARTHA: Carry-bed 41 marks, four bedcovers for the baby
carriage at 10.90 apiece is 43.60, a basket for underneath
the baby carriage, three bedcovers, pillows, two pillowcases,
bath towel, two covered pails for the bathroom . . . wait a
minute, that's part of the other section already. So,
depending on quality, washables run around 80 marks for
the average stuff and a hundred for the first-class kind.

KURT: For 20 marks? Get the first-class kind.

MARTHA: That's what I thought too. Next: covered pails for
the bathroom, 9.90 apiece is 19.80, soapdish 3.35,
hairbrush and comb for baby 10.25, baby's bath
thermometer 3.80, a changing stand 48.50, a bathtub
15.30, a bathtub stand makes the tub more practical,
32.50, a bottle-holder 7.50. Question: should we get an
electric bottle-warmer, they cost 26.80 and they're not
necessary but they save a lot of time.

KURT: You got time if you're not working.

MARTHA: Well, but there's my piecework . . .

KURT: Is that typical, a bottle-warmer?

MARTHA: Not typical, only when people can afford it.

KURT *(Thinks it over)*: You got it.

MARTHA: They're really better! Six Aleta brand wide-mouth
bottles with screw-tops at 2.95 each is 17.70, a large
economy size bottle of disinfectant, 11.80, oops, wait,
that should be with the health supplies after we're home
from the hospital. . . . I need a nursing bra, 20 marks
90, a maternity dress for dress-up 160.80 and one for
everyday 58.10 and a maternity suit which is more
practical, 125. So . . .

KURT: You got 'em.

MARTHA: Now we get to the problems. Adele will let us have the crib coverlet, the crib mattress and one baby blanket used . . .

KURT: My baby don't need anything used.

MARTHA: That's what I thought, but the things are still in good shape . . .

KURT: No.

MARTHA: Fine. Coverlet about 40 marks, mattress 22.80 and a premium baby blanket 45. Oh, *here's* something: "Trimskin, for the prevention of stretch marks?!" It's supposed to be very good but it's very expensive.

KURT: Stretch marks?

MARTHA: You get these red marks on your legs and stomach, this "Trimskin" prevents them, but it's 9.90 a bottle.

KURT: That's OK.

MARTHA: But a bottle lasts only about ten days and it's high time I was using it already, I should already have started.

KURT: Get started, we don't want you getting stretched; maybe if you're careful you can make a bottle last two weeks.

MARTHA: Good, so I'll look good again after it's born.

KURT: You look good now. But stretches would be bad.

MARTHA: I agree.

KURT: 'Cause I'm proud of you.

MARTHA: Don't worry. I'm taking care of myself. They say being pregnant is like a purifying bath for a woman, especially when it's a boy.

KURT: It's a boy, you can tell.

MARTHA: Yes. . . . Let's keep going, this is important. You don't *have* to have a diaper cabinet, but there are some extra nice ones that really look like something. Should we?

KURT: How much?

MARTHA: It depends. The one I've got my eye on isn't cheap.

KURT: That's because you got taste that's out of the ordinary. Remember that time you were looking to find a tie to go with that new suit and the way you just reached into the rack of ties and pulled one out?

Martha nods.

And how the salesman said: "Your wife has got a remarkable eye for quality! That one's more expensive than average, but it's exquisite." That's what he said.

MARTHA: It *is* a pretty tie.

KURT: Uh-huh.

MARTHA: Should I buy the diaper cabinet I mentioned? It costs 245 marks, after all . . .

KURT *(Looks at her. Smiles. Nods)*: You got it!

MARTHA: Good. Now this question is really serious: *(Pause. She sniffs)* Should we use normal wash-and-wear diapers for the baby or disposables?

Kurt looks at her uncertainly.

I said it was a problem! Modern households use disposable diapers these days, because it's sanitary and because of saving so much time it's got advantages. They're called "Pampers" and they're famous.

KURT: Well, if they got advantages?!'

MARTHA: But I'm not sure yet, because the old things have their uses, and they're not cheap, Pampers aren't, 6.60 for 30 of them, and the baby's got to be changed six or seven times a day. But keeping supplied with diapers isn't so cheap either, the real kind that you wash. And if I don't have so much work to do I can make more ties.

KURT: We can come up with everything we need and what's

respectable, that's all taken care of, without you making any ties.

MARTHA: I'd rather have the modern diapers. They're actually recommended.

KURT: Then take 'em. You got 'em!

MARTHA: Fine. *(Writes)* Then we need over-diapers and pads, that's normal. *(Writes)*

KURT: OK.

MARTHA: That's what we need to start off with.

KURT: That's all?

MARTHA *(Laughs)*: I haven't counted in medicine to start with, but you have to figure on 150 marks. And I've already bought 75 marks' worth of knitting wool and I've used up maybe 25 marks' worth, not more than that, because I've got this piece work now. Oh and I bought this book about the baby in the womb and then another one for after it's born.

KURT: So we'll know what we're doing.

MARTHA: Exactly, and the doctor suggested it. *(Sniffs)* That's it, unless we think of something else.

KURT: You can put something down for me there too: a flash attachment for 79.90, five rolls of film, 5.50 each, and developing for 19 marks 80. *(Laughs)* We're going to get this down from the first day on!

MARTHA *(Laughs too)*: I would have forgotten all about that!

KURT: Not me! *(Looks at list)* Let me figure it up, I'm good at it.

MARTHA: There.

Kurt adds it all together, enjoying the process. Martha watches with pleasure.

It's a lot, you'll see!

KURT: It's all been authorized already, don't worry.

(Calculates) Two thousand seven hundred and twelve-fifty.

MARTHA: Three thousand, I thought when you add in the things you forgot and you remember later.

KURT: Three thousand. *(Pause)* I told my relief driver, a kid costs you four thousand, just to start with.

MARTHA: Once it's born, there'll be more bills to pay, that's obvious.

KURT: I can handle it. *(Nods)* No problem.

SCENE FOUR

In an allotment garden,[1] *very small, spic and span. Kurt and Martha are setting out plants.*

KURT *(Holds one plant)*: Top's broken off. Too bad.

MARTHA: It's nice-looking anyway.

KURT: Thank God for that, it cost enough.

MARTHA: But they're beautiful. *(Straightens up)*

KURT: Tired?

MARTHA *(Nods, smiles)*: Yes. *(Short pause)* You'd hardly know me, would you? The least little thing and I'm worn out.

KURT: You think I'm so dumb I got no consideration for your condition. Sit down and rest, I'll do the rest myself.

MARTHA: A little anyway.

KURT: As long as you like.

Martha leaves the flowerbeds and sits down on a garden chair on the little terrace. Long pause. Martha watches Kurt as he goes on working, setting out the little plants lovingly, with the greatest exactness and care. Pause.

MARTHA *(Smiling)*: The original Green Thumb.

KURT: I always been like this.

MARTHA: I know.

KURT: When my dad come that time and said, "We're going to give the garden up 'cause we're old now, you want it? I'd like you to have it, 'cause then I'd know it was in good hands." I didn't even have to think it over, I just said, "You bet! Sure!"

MARTHA: You did the right thing. *(Pause)* Know what I'm thinking about?

KURT *(Looks at her)*: Nope.

MARTHA: Something in particular.

KURT: What am I, a fortune-teller? (*Short pause*) But I got an idea. *(Laughs)*

MARTHA: Think you're smart.

KURT: You're thinking about love. *(Martha laughs. Kurt points at her belly)* For that in there.

MARTHA: That's right.

KURT: So what *were* you thinking?

MARTHA: I was thinking, it won't be long, he'll be running around the garden while we sit here and watch and feel good.

KURT: I was just thinking the same myself. *(Short pause)* We'll have to let him see right from the beginning how things have to be. No screwing around. You got to start early and show where the flowers are and how you got to walk on the board between the beds, and where you can run around any way you like. 'Cause it'd be a shame if everything got trampled on.

MARTHA: Nothing's going to get trampled on by our baby, I'm not worried.

KURT: "As the twig is bent, so grows the tree. . . ."² *(Short pause)* What I thought I'd do is I'd build a sandbox, only I don't know where to put it yet. Because sand is bad for

a garden, especially a small one like ours, and you throw
sand around it's going to be ruined before you know it.

MARTHA: But there has to be a sandbox.

KURT: Said I'm going to build one. Only where? First I
think, right by the patio, then you always got an eye on
what's going on.

MARTHA: What's the matter with that?

KURT: 'Cause it's right by the beds is why, and if you always
got to be getting down on him that's no good either.

MARTHA: Well, it's necessary to teach them what's allowed
and what isn't.

KURT: I guess. I thought maybe I could make a little fence
around the beds, it wouldn't have to be very high, then
we could relax.

MARTHA: That doesn't look very nice, a fence . . . and
anyway, the baby should do what he's supposed to
because that's the way things ought to be and not just
because of a fence. Life's a lot easier if you learn to play
by the rules and not go getting into situations every
time you turn around.

KURT: That's true, too.

Pause. Kurt goes on working. Martha sits watching him. Pause.

Not everybody's got their own garden, you got to learn
to value what you got!

MARTHA: That's right.

Pause.

SCENE FIVE

*In Kurt and Martha's apartment. Martha is making dinner. Kurt,
wearing a pullover sweater, is flipping through a thick magazine devoted
to the new automobile models.*

MARTHA: You notice anything different?

KURT: What?

MARTHA: If you notice anything. *(Pause)* You feel
  uncomfortable maybe?

KURT: Why should I?

MARTHA: Got an itch you can't scratch?

KURT: No!

MARTHA *(Smiles)*: I got a confession to make. Since we
  starting saving up on account of the bubbi, I been saving
  on household expenses too.

KURT: A little here, a little there'll do it.

MARTHA: That's right, and so I don't use "Softy" any more
  for your sweaters. *(Short pause)* You know: "Mothers: is
  your conscience clear?"

KURT: Advertising!

MARTHA: That's right: "Make your woollens baby-lamb-
  soft." But since we got to save somewhere I thought
  leave the stuff out for once and see what happens. Your
  sweater itch you?

KURT: Not at all.

MARTHA: Then I'm glad, and *(Laughs a little)* so I don't
  have to have a guilty conscience?

KURT: No.

MARTHA: There's a few other things I figured out where I
  could save, you'll find out.

KURT: I'm bringing everything I said I would, you don't
  have to save on the washing for Pete's sake!

MARTHA: Now be nice, remember I'm pregnant!

KURT: It's all only for you and the kid anyway! *(Short pause)* The boss takes an interest, you got to give him that much, he understands the situation. How much you think I take in this week?

MARTHA: A lot.

KURT: You bet I did, this week I put in sixty-three hours, that's something, and next week I'm at the head of the overtime list again. Thank God for it!

MARTHA: They know we need the money.

KURT: The boss says don't let it get around. *(Smiles)* Look here at this, will you?

MARTHA: What?

KURT: He finally got it, and he's been waiting months on it already.

Martha comes over and looks at the magazine.

His new car. "Iso Rivolta Fidia 300," eight cylinders, fifty-three hundred fifty-nine cc, 300 horsepower, overhead valves, gravity-feed dual carburetors, fully-synchronized four-speed transmission, optional automatic, independent front suspension, De Dion rear axle, hydraulic damping, positraction, top speed two hundred and twenty kilometers per hour! *(Looks up, smiles, nods)* The boss knows something about cars, no Mercedes or something that everybody's got for him, no: lso Rivolta, something to make everybody look and eat their heart out.

MARTHA: What did that cost?

KURT *(Reads)*: "Price: about sixty thousand marks!"

MARTHA: The magazine, I mean!

KURT: It's got every car in the world in it! Six marks.

MARTHA: Expensive, when we're supposed to be economizing.

KURT: A person's got a right to a little enjoyment.

MARTHA: It's time we ate.

KURT: Some day we're going to buy our own car, you know; sometime later.

MARTHA: We ought to be thinking about the baby now.

KURT: What else we doing? But later, when we got some breathing space!

MARTHA: Then, fine, but first *(Smiles)* three weeks now, if it's on time! *(Sniffs. Laughs)* Eat!

SCENE SIX

At the hospital. Martha lies in bed with the baby in her arm. Kurt stands beside the bed with flowers. Long pause. Martha radiant. Kurt looking at her.

MARTHA *(Softly)*: Here he is.

> *Kurt nods.*

Your son. *(Pause)* See him?

> *Kurt nods. Pause.*

You like him?

> *Kurt nods. Martha laughs.*

KURT: Yes. *(Smiles, nods, looks at her, begins to cry)* Yes.

Act Two

SCENE ONE

In the kitchen. Kurt has Stefan on his lap, playing "Church-Tower"
with him. Martha is busy with her tie-knitting, which she is naturally
very good at by now.

KURT *(To Stefan, high voice)*: And the little bell goes: *(Swings*
Stefan back and forth) Ding-ding-ding-ding-ding-ding-
ding-ding. *(Now in a deeper voice)* And now the big bell
goes: *(Swings Stefan back and forth, slowly)* Ding, dong,
ding, dong, ding, dong, ding, dong, ding, dong, ding,
dong, ding, dong. . . . *(Very deep voice)* And now the
great great great big bell goes: *(Swings Stefan back and*
forth very slowly) Bong . . . Dong . . . Bong . . . Dong
. . . Bong . . . Dong . . . Bong . . . Dong . . . Bong . . .
Dong . . . Bong . . . Dong . . . Bong . . . Dong. . . .
(Very high voice) And now the itty-tiny little bell!
(Shakes Stefan back and forth as fast as he can) Dinga-
linga-linga-linga-linga-linga-linga. *(And so on. Gives*

Stefan a kiss) You're your Daddy's big boy, you know
that? His pride and joy, like they say.

MARTHA *(Smiling)*: What about me?

KURT: You too!

SCENE TWO

*A lovely, secluded clearing by a little lake. Beautiful day. Martha and
Kurt enter on bicycles. Stefan rides on a kiddy-seat with Kurt.*

KURT: You got to know your way around, right?

MARTHA: And such a beautiful day!

KURT: Sure is.

> *They dismount from their bikes, spread out a blanket, a little seat
> for Stefan, unpack various things, etc. Then they take off their
> outer clothing. They're already wearing their bathing gear. They
> stretch out in the sun, etc.*

MARTHA: 'v'I got my figure back? *(Smiles)* My bathing suit
fits as good as before. Not every woman can say that.

KURT *(Looking proudly at her)*: You're entitled.

MARTHA: See any stretches?

KURT: Not a one. Everything's just like always.

MARTHA: Don't want a new model?

KURT: Never.

MARTHA: That's what I like to hear! *(Snuggles up beside him.
Pause)* It's like a little piece of paradise.

KURT: You got to know where to look.

MARTHA: Who needs a car when the most beautiful places
are right in your front yard.

KURT: Only if you know your way around.

MARTHA: And we know our way around. You do.

Pause.

KURT: Later on I'll build the kid a castle with a moat around it.

MARTHA: He's too young for that.

KURT: He can watch then, learn something. *(Turns to baby)* Right? *(Stefan squeaks contentedly. Pause. Quietly)* But I wish I was working right now, anyway! *(Smiles)* But if there ain't no work to do, you can't do nothing about it.

MARTHA: You can take one Saturday off, you've been at it a year.

KURT: We need it or not?

MARTHA: I said back then, there'd be lots of extras afterwards.

KURT: When they say a kid's expensive they're not kidding.

MARTHA: You ought to be glad, not everybody can handle it like we can.

KURT: If there was more work around, it still would be better.

MARTHA: Enjoy the day; maybe you won't see such a nice one soon again.

KURT: Right.

SCENE THREE

In the bedroom (bed, baby bed, etc.); deep night. Kurt snorts and talks incomprehensibly in his sleep. Martha wakes up.

MARTHA: Kurtie? *(Shakes him)* What's the matter, Kurtie?

Kurt awakens with a jolt.

What is it?

KURT: Wha-?

MARTHA: You were carrying on in your sleep like a wild man.

KURT: Why?

MARTHA: How do I know?

Pause. Kurt pulls himself together.

KURT: Dreaming, 'sgetting to be. . . . Like I'm driving and I see the load has come adrift, you understand, sliding forward over the cab, I can't stop, on the freeway or somewhere, down over the edge. *(Short pause)* Lot of crap, a load coming adrift like that, it's happened sometimes in other companies, right, but not in our shop—not a chance. *(Laughs)*

MARTHA: No.

KURT: I wake you up?

MARTHA *(Lying)*: I was awake.

KURT: So. *(Short pause)* We probably ate too much. Mayonnaise can be heavy on the stomach, I heard that.

MARTHA: I made the salad just like always. The salads I make are always digestible.

KURT: All right, it was the turkey, then. *(Laughs)*

MARTHA: You're working yourself too hard, Kurtie, that's what it is. Can't let one job go.

KURT: Darn right I don't. *(Pause)* Got everything we need! . . . You missing out on something?

MARTHA: What?

KURT: There's all kinds of stuff a man can give a woman.

MARTHA: You do what you can.

Short pause.

KURT: Other guys earn more than I do.

MARTHA: I'm satisfied.

KURT: Or they get the same, only without no overtime. At home more. *(Smiles)*

MARTHA: How a man earns a living is his business. The main thing is it's here.

KURT *(Laughs, nods)*: And it's there! *(Pause)* Nearly 1400 take-home, month after month too! *(Nods)* If you was married to a section chief you probably wouldn't see any more.

MARTHA: No.

KURT: Yep. *(Pause)* Course, if the overtime don't keep up like it's been but falls off on account of this recession or whatever, that's bad.

MARTHA: You'll manage, I'm sure.

KURT: Yeah, how? *(Pause)* Your civil servant, now, he don't have to worry, the economic situation don't affect him, it's all the same whatever happens, that's the difference.

MARTHA: Everybody can't be a civil servant.

KURT: No. *(Pause)* The foreigners, you know, the Turks and Eye-Ties, the boss says they're getting the zip one after the other. *(Short pause)* You know what I'm talking about? They're laying off.

MARTHA: But you're no foreigner!

KURT: Thank God for that. *(Pause)* First the foreigners get it, then the rest of us, that's what some of them are saying around the plant.

MARTHA: That's a lot of foolishness. Anyway, if they fired everybody else the boss'd keep *you* on.

KURT: 'Cause he likes me, right. *(Short pause)* 'Cause I mind my own business and just think about the job. He likes to see that, he told me. He says he wishes everybody was like me. *(Pause, smiles)* No, we don't got to be concerned; 'cause before I start to feel like I'm getting close to the edge, all the rest'll be long gone already. *(Smiles)*

MARTHA: 'Cause the boss likes you, 'cause you're dependable and never make trouble.

KURT: Damn right.

Pause.

MARTHA: You're sweating like anything!
KURT: 'Cause I'm hot.

SCENE FOUR

In the allotment garden. Kurt is building a sandbox. Martha is working among the flowerbeds. Stefan plays. Long pause while they work.

MARTHA: I'm going to lie down a while in the lounge chair, get some sun.
KURT: Fine. I'm going to finish the frame, then I'll get to work on the beds.
MARTHA: You take a break too! You have to enjoy the summer while you can!
KURT: I get plenty of enjoyment just from doing something. Tomorrow's the first Saturday in a month when I can get in some overtime again. *(Laughs)* Just me, all alone, the boss says.
MARTHA: What is it?
KURT: Special assignment!

Laughs. Martha stretches out in the deck chair.

Thank God!

Goes on working. Pause.

SCENE FIVE

The idyllic clearing by the little lake (same as Act Two, Scene Two), a beautiful day. Sound of a heavy truck driving up. Motor cut off. Pause.

Kurt enters, looking around, smiles, goes again. He reenters with a barrel, opens the tap, and lets a brownish-red fluid run into the lake. He doesn't act at all fearful about this, rather triumphant, unquestioning. Kurt takes the empty barrel back with him, returns with a full one. This set of actions is repeated eight times. While the last barrel is draining, Kurt stands by the little lake looking around at the scenery. Then he notices the sandcastle (a very beautiful one) which he presumably built for Stefan earlier.

KURT: Out of sight, out of mind. Exactly.

Kurt smiles, takes the last barrel, and exits. Sound of a heavy truck starting, gearing up, driving off, disappearing in the distance. Great stillness. . . . Long pause.

Martha enters on the bicycle, with Stefan in the baby-carrier on the handlebars. She parks the bike, takes Stefan out, spreads out a blanket, etc., arranges everthing, sits down on the blanket with Stefan without undressing.

MARTHA: If Daddy could see us through a telescope, wouldn't he be proud to see how we can take care of ourselves? A good Daddy who works morning to night so his family has everything they need. *(Looks at the child)* Our Daddy is a *good* Daddy. Are you hot? You want Mommy to go swimming with you? Hm? Splash, splish, great big fish?

Martha laughs, gets undressed, bathing suit already on under, takes all of little Stefan's clothes off. They play together, then she carries the baby to the water's edge.

Look at the castle Daddy made specially for you, it's still there, because nobody knows about our secret place!

Martha goes into the water with the baby on her arm; she stands finally up to her waist in the water, then she dips Stefan in a little, splashes him a little, dips him in a little, then more, etc., splashing with him. Pause. The baby begins to yell mightily, Martha is startled.

Silly baby, afraid of the water. . . . It won't bite you! The fishies are in the water day and night, even when they're little baby fishies, and they swim like anything . . . and you're a little fraidy-cat!

Martha dips him in the water again, this time more cautiously; the child screams even louder, more fearfully.

What's the matter with you? Now, now, baby boy! We'll get right out again if he doesn't want to swim today, right this minute!

Martha carries Stefan out of the water to the blanket, lays him down; the child continues to scream terribly.

It's all over, it's all over, there's no water any more, just the nice sun, go on with you, crying like that just because of a few drops of water! *(Pause. She tries to calm the child by picking it up and rocking it in her arms)* The big bell, pay attention now: ding, dong, ding, dong, ding, dong . . . and now the middle-size bell, ring-ding, ring-ding, ring-ding, ring-ding, ring-ding, ring-ding . . . and now the itty-bitty tiny bell, dinga-linga-linga-linga-linga-linga-linga-ling . . . and now the great *great* big bell. Dong . . . dong . . . dongle-ong, dongle-ong . . . for God's sake poops, what is it?

Stefan has become boiled-crab red; now he goes blue all over his whole body.

Why are you going all blue, that's a fine state of affairs! *(Softly)* Stefan, poopsie—oh my God, a baby that turns blue is in danger, it's in the book, big letters and underlined, it's choking on something.

Martha jumps up, pulls her clothes on quickly, leaves everything lying, throws something around the baby, puts it in its seat, and rides quickly away.

SCENE SIX

In the apartment. Kurt sits staring at Martha: she's cried herself into exhaustion; she has wrapped light gauze bandages around her legs. It is afternoon.

MARTHA: We have to wait, they said at the clinic, see how bad the burns are or not. *(A crying fit overtakes her. Kurt sits and stares)* It's not so serious for me because I'm grown up. *(Pause)* Criminals, poisoning the water in our secret place with . . . poison, where no one knows about it . . . they didn't even spoil the castle you built.

Pause.

KURT: Why'd you go out there without me to take care of you?

MARTHA: What?

KURT: Without me, 'cause you're not safe without me, 'cause I know my way around.

MARTHA: Why . . . ?

Pause.

KURT *(Softly)*: 'Cause it was me, with the poison. *(Short pause)* This afternoon.

Martha looks at him. Pause.

SCENE SEVEN

It has become evening. The situation is unchanged. Martha is by the stove. Great silence.

KURT: I feel like not even human. Me.

MARTHA: I don't know how you can talk. Murderer.

KURT: I guess you don't want any more to do with me now, huh? *(Long pause)* If I could I would change places this second and it'd be me in the hospital. But it don't work that way. *(Smiles shamefacedly)*

MARTHA: How can a man like you laugh?

KURT: I wasn't laughing at all.

MARTHA: You were.

KURT: It was a mistake.

Long pause.

MARTHA: Just be quiet, I said.

KURT *(Though he has said nothing)*: OK. *(Pause)* It's no go with us now, huh?

MARTHA: It's finished.

KURT: Yes. *(Pause)* No one can live with a man who murdered his own kid. What if he comes through, though?

MARTHA: You better hope.

Long pause.

KURT *(Softly)*: Martha? *(Martha is silent. Long pause)* 's there something to eat?

MARTHA: Not for you.

KURT: No.

MARTHA: I'll never share a table with you again.

KURT: I'll sit somewheres else.

MARTHA: Otherwise I won't go near the table.

KURT: I'm gone already.

Kurt sits in a corner. Pause. Martha serves up food for herself. Pause. Martha eats.

Hope it's good!

MARTHA *(Looking at him)* A man like you, say that kind of thing.

KURT: Sorry. *(Pause)* You feel sick just looking at me, huh?

MARTHA: Yes.

KURT: Me too.

Long pause. Martha eats. Kurt watches, suddenly begins to yell.

Wine! Wine! Wine, he said, the boss, gone bad, nothing dangerous about it, the fish'll get drunk and have themselves a ball, that's it! *(Yelling louder)* Take it someplace where no one knows about, the boss said, it's the pure food laws, there's nothing dangerous about spoiled wine but they can fine you anyway. That's why I took it to our place, for the boss, sure enough, you can count on me, all he's got to do is give me the word, I'm his boy! *(He begins to be overcome by weeping, pounding himself on the chest)* A good worker, special assignment, carried out according to specifications. *(Reaches into his breast pocket)* Hundred marks extra, there! *(He howls. Pause. Loudly)* The boss said . . .

MARTHA *(Screaming)*: The boss said! And I suppose if the boss said, "Bring me your baby's head, it won't hurt the baby, but I'll give you a hundred marks for it," I suppose you'd do that too, because the boss said so, right? *(Short pause, then more quietly)* You're not a human being at all, I guess I just never noticed before; you're nothing but a well-trained ape! That boss of yours is a criminal, that's all, but I'm not married to him, I'm married to you. And it's not easy for a woman to admit she wasted her best years on something like you.

KURT: On a trained ape?

MARTHA: Exactly. *(She emits a shuddering noise of rejection and disgust, pulls herself together)* So: now I'm going to the clinic to see how Stefan is; you do what you like.

Exit. Kurt looks after her. Pause.

SCENE EIGHT

The clearing. The bathing things are still lying just as Martha left them. Evening.

Kurt arrives on his bicycle. He comes to the bathing things, sets his bike aside. Pause. He looks around, uncertain, embarrassed.

Slowly he moves his head, looks to the left and the right, nods sometimes without motivation, etc.

Then he picks all the things up Martha left behind. He folds them carefully up, the blanket, etc. He picks up a little toy bear of Stefan's, looks at it, carefully adds it to the pile. He stows everything on the carrier of his bike. Takes the satchel that's hanging on the handlebars, takes (out) a large carton, pair of scissors, a marker. He cuts a sign-sized piece out of the carton, lays it on the ground, writes on it with the marker: "No swimming! Caution! Poison! Danger!" He has to draw over the letters again and again to make them broad enough.

Then he goes to the bike and takes a broomstick that he has tied lengthwise on the frame, gets more tools out of the satchel. He nails the sign to the broomstick. Then he digs a hole in the bank and rams the broomstick with the sign on it into the hole. He fills the hole with

*earth, tamps it down, etc. This work takes a long time, it's done
very meticulously, almost pedantically.*

*Only when all is complete and he is certain that the sign can't be
overlooked does he take his bike and ride off.*

Pause.

*Kurt returns. He remains sitting on the bike by the shore. Looks
into the water.*

Long pause.

*Kurt nods to himself, first slightly, then more firmly. He sets the
bike aside, begins slowly to get undressed, down to his underpants,
which he leaves on. He lays his clothes neatly beside the bike. Then
he goes very slowly to the water, goes in, to the middle.*

Pause.

*Kurt looks around. Then he ducks down, first up to his neck, then
over his head, so he can't be seen any more. He remains under a long
time. Then he stands up again, waits, and goes back to the shore.*

Pause.

*He looks down at himself. Tries to see changes. There aren't any,
though. Kurt goes back in the water, dives under again, comes back
out. In the meantime he has begun to shiver violently, for it is cool
out. He waits, inspects his skin, nothing. Shivering, he dries himself
with a hand towel Martha left behind, gets dressed again. Looks
around. Makes a helpless gesture.*

Pause.

Act Three

SCENE ONE

Darkness. The apartment door opens. Light is switched on. Kurt enters. Very slowly, quietly. He closes the door(s) behind him. His face and hands are slightly reddened; the area around his eyes is bright red. He remains standing. Looks around.

Pause.

He goes into the living room, switches on the light. Goes into the bedroom, switches the light on here too. Looks around. Waits. He shudders, although there's no reason for him to. He goes back into the kitchen. Stays standing by the door.

Long pause.

Kurt goes to the dresser, opens a drawer and takes some pieces of rope out. He tests them with a professional air and puts them away again.

Pause.

He has an idea. He goes into the hall and gets an old-fashioned washing-line winder there. Brings it into the kitchen. Sits down at the table and begins to unwind the line. He's economical with the line, trying to imagine how much will do. He stands up, goes to the dresser, gets out a scissors, cuts the line off. He tests it, pulls on it. He takes the cut-off part of the line and lays it out along the remainder. Measures off the same length, cuts off another length, ties the two together at the ends so he has a double length. Lays the line on the table. He takes the line-bobbin with the rest of the line on it back to its place in the hall. Returns, puts the scissors back in the dresser.

Pause.

He takes the double line and stands there. Looks around. He doesn't know what to do next. He goes through the whole apartment. Looks for something solid to hang from. Finds nothing. Comes back into the kitchen. Goes to the kitchen window, takes the curtain rod with its drawn curtains down. Jumps when he realizes that now people can see him from outside. Puts the curtain back up quickly, pulls the opening carefully shut.

Pause.

Goes into the toilet. It's the modern kind without a high water reservoir. He comes back. This scene should last a very long time.

Long pause.

Kurt gives up on hanging himself. He puts the rope on the kitchen table. He goes to the dresser, takes out various medicines, puts them on the table. There's nothing there to die with.

Pause.

Kurt goes into the bathroom and gets his razor, carries it into the kitchen, sets it on the table. Sits down. Takes the used blade out of the apparatus. Tests it. Puts it back in.

Pause.

Takes a new blade out of its packaging. Holds it a long time in his hand. Looks at it. He begins to perspire.

Pause.

Kurt looks around. Stands up and turns out the lights all through the apartment.

Darkness. You can hear him coming back into the kitchen. Sitting down.

Very long pause.

After a long time you can hear Kurt standing up. He turns the light on again. There are tears in his eyes. He's just about done in. He begins to put the medicines away again.

Pause.

He takes his razor and is about to put it away. Apartment door opens. Martha enters.

MARTHA *(Calling)*: Kurtie? He's out of danger! Kurt? *(Comes into the kitchen)* Kurtie?

KURT *(Fearful, smiling, soft, quick)*: Just shaving!

MARTHA *(Looks at him, uncertain)*: What's wrong with your . . . ?

KURT: I went in the water too. See what it was like.

MARTHA: I see. *(Pause. Goes to table, sees the medicine bottles and the rope; uncertainly)* No sense of order.

Very long pause.

KURT: I can't stand being around myself, Martha. On account of.

Long pause.

MARTHA: He's out of danger, Kurtie, Stefan is.

KURT: Yes.

MARTHA: In two or three days he can come home again. He got off easy.

KURT: Yes.

Pause.

MARTHA: Aren't you glad? That your son's on the way to recovery?

KURT: Course I am. Sure.

Very long pause.

MARTHA: A decent person doesn't kill himself when there's no reason to.

KURT: Yes.

Pause.

MARTHA: You just got taken in because you're a good man who's not suspicious. . . . It's the boss's fault, not yours.

KURT: Yes.

MARTHA: How were you supposed to know he was lying to you, he's always taken such an interest in us. And suddenly something like this! You can't figure on something like that happening.

KURT: No.

Long pause.

MARTHA: A man as good as you would be hard to find. Look around and see what all you done.

KURT: Yes.

MARTHA: Because you're a hard worker! *(Pause)* Stefan needs his papa! *(Pause)* Killing yourself is a sin! *(Short pause)* Kurtie!

Pause.

KURT: I didn't come close to doing it. I been at it an hour already. *(Pause)* How's a trained ape going to kill himself, anyway?

MARTHA: That got you, huh? That I said that. I'm sorry.

KURT: But it's true just the same.

MARTHA: Don't be silly!

KURT *(Gently)*: Don't lie, now. *(Pause)* I'm one of your . . . what do you call it . . . your blunt instruments. *(Smiles. Pause)*

MARTHA: You're no different than most people!

KURT: If somebody told me a couple days ago what I'm like I wouldn't have believed him . . . I would have laughed my head off. *(Pause)* That's what it is. *(Short pause)* A revelation what you call. *(Pause)* I don't want to have nothing to do with myself, after what I know. When you look in the mirror you think, that can't be me. Him!?

MARTHA: But we need you, Kurtie.

KURT: The man who kills his kids?

MARTHA: I'm sorry I said that.

KURT: You said it.

MARTHA: I know. I'm sorry. Forget it.

KURT: Even if it's the truth?

MARTHA: It's not.

KURT: Because he's still alive, the kid?

MARTHA: And because it wasn't intentional, it was a mistake.

Pause.

KURT: It wasn't any mistake, Martha. That's just it. Somebody like me, they just send him out in the morning like a little kid going to the store. How far would they have to go to get a "no" out of me? What all can they tell me to do? No, it wasn't no mistake. That's how I am. *(Pause)* There's all kinds of stuff they want people to do, Martha! And his kind *(Points to himself)* is the kind that does it.

MARTHA: Not you, I know you better than that. You're a good man, no one can tell me different, not even you. You're ready and willing, that's you. . . . Look around at everything you been able to do just because you're a decent person *(Momentarily high diction)* with the sweat of your brow. Then you'll start thinking different. . . . Start at the beginning! Don't you remember? *(Smiles)* The most up-to-date baby carriage there is, a Paidi-Bed, clothes good enough for a little prince, semi-private room in the hospital, *(Nods)* fur coat for me when I come home, Persian lamb with a real mink collar, just now a new washing machine, and it won't be long until we have a new color TV . . .

KURT *(Roaring)*: No! *(Long pause)* Tomorrow early I'm going to the police and turning myself in. The boss and me both.

Martha looks at him.

SCENE TWO

In the bedroom at night. Kurt and Martha are in the marriage bed; it is dark.

MARTHA *(Softly)*: Can't you act as if it was a mistake that never happened. And watch out the next time?

KURT: Would I really be straight with you again then, after everything that's happened? *(Short pause)* Martha?

MARTHA: You ought to go on living and not get us into an awful mess.

KURT: But you want me different, don't you?

MARTHA: Oh, a little, maybe; if a person could choose . . .

KURT: OK, I want to be different too. Because right now I'm not a man, or anyway only the way you say it without thinking. *(Pause)* Back, Martha, I can't never go back. *(Shakes his head)* I'd rather be dead. And if I try ten times, one way's sure to work.

MARTHA: Only thinking of yourself.

KURT: How can I face up to the kid, the way things are? "It was a mistake, honey, but it won't happen again, 'cause how often would the boss have a 'special assignment' like that?" *(Pause)* No, Martha, it can't just go on this way. I want to . . . unload, tear out the weeds, I want to . . . and you have to help, please!

MARTHA: I'm afraid.

KURT: I am too. . . . If I go and tell everything and hang the boss, then I'm out of a job tomorrow, and I won't get a new one fast around here, the boss'll see to that. That's for sure.

MARTHA: Then we can just move away, Kurt, somewhere where no one knows us! Then it'll all be over. You have to think about that.

Pause.

KURT: Martha, nobody can blame us for being like we were,
you and me. Them over us, they seen to it that we never
really woke up and started living, like they say. We can
prove that easy, anytime. But Martha, if we go on like
that now, in this situation, just stick our heads back in
the sand, then we're just as bad this time ourselves, we
can't shove it off on somebody else. That's what it is.

MARTHA: Well, be brave, Kurtie. It's going to be tough,
though.

KURT: I know. . . . You going to help me anyway?

MARTHA: Don't know, if I can.

Pause.

KURT: Look, Martha, try to see: I can't never be somebody's
illusion, but a man you can have some respect for, he's
got to have something inside.

MARTHA: I know. The illusion was, I don't know, not just
handsome, or rich, but . . .

KURT: Not a trained ape, anyhow. *(Martha is silent)* If you
can help, I can do it, I'm sure.

MARTHA: I'm your wife. What use to me is a husband who
wants to kill himself, I'd rather have one who gets some
joy out of life, I got to consider that. But it's still tough,
just the same. *(Pause)* But who knows, you never can tell
until you try. How's a swan going to know he's a swan if
he spends all his time with the ducks, like in the old
story. *(Short pause)* Go to sleep now, you need your
strength in the morning.

KURT: Yes.

SCENE THREE

Early morning in the kitchen. At breakfast. Kurt is wearing his nicest suit. Martha in bathrobe.

MARTHA: Eat something solid, it'll keep you calm.

KURT: If I don't have to throw up; I feel sick already.

MARTHA: Want a shot of schnapps to settle your stomach?

KURT: Then for sure the boss'll say I'm drunk and better go sober up first. *(Smiles)* Scared to death already, huh?

MARTHA: You're all right. *(Short pause)* I just thought of something! When I was a kid in school we had a teacher we were scared of. An art teacher. *(Laughs)* Once I had to go up in front of the class and I managed to knock over a bottle of ink, acccidentally, you know. And he gave me such a whipping in front of the class that I wet my pants. All wet, my dress too, and I had to sit like that until school was out. *(Short pause)* I was so ashamed you can't imagine! *(Shakes her head)* When I told them at home what happened my father gave me a clout or two himself. I'll never forget that.

Pause.

KURT: So?

MARTHA: Nothing, it just occurred to me.

KURT: Memories, huh.

MARTHA: Yes.

Pause.

KURT: I'll go now.

MARTHA: All right.

Kurt stands up, pulls his coat on, looks at her. Martha nods. Exit Kurt.

SCENE FOUR

In the kitchen. Martha and Kurt. Midday.

KURT: First he jumped all over me 'cause I dumped it where
somebody could go swimming. He called me an idiot.
Then he said it had to be a mistake about it being
poison. These days everything is separated out and safe
he said.

MARTHA: What did you say?

KURT: I said I was going to the cops and tell them
everything. What he did and what I did. *(Pause)* Then
he started screaming. Like a wild man! Said I was
drunk, right, even though I didn't have that schnapps.
At first when he was yelling at me I was scared, but then
I wasn't anymore. *(Smiles)* You get used to being yelled
at. I told him I was ready to take on the responsibility
for what I did, he ought to come along to the police and
admit his part of it. Then he got real pale, right, and
said what was I talking about taking responsibility.
Someone like me don't have any assets to be responsible
with, he said, what does the law care about a clown like
me, they're going to go after whoever's got the bucks. So
I said to him, they got no use for a trained ape, huh?
(Laughs) He thought about that a minute, and then he
asked who put me up to it. *(Pause)* And that's when I
lied, *(Smiles)* and told him "plenty of people." *(Pause)*
'Cause I didn't want to feel all alone. What you call a
white lie, right, you can't blame me for that. *(Short
pause)* And the effect that had on him, you couldn't
describe it. No more screaming from then on, instead he
got like totally polite. Well, he said, let's see now. Very
formal. Before I went he was offering me favors. He'd set

everything up with the hospital he said, said he knows the director personally, take care of the expenses and see to it we got compensation. Stick to him and we won't be sorry. But if I really went to the cops he said he'd see to it not only I got canned but I'd never get another job anywhere. Because of his connections. I might just as well hang myself right off. *(Pause. Softly)* But the way he said it, Martha, I could tell he was scared. He didn't believe it himself. *(Nods; pause)* I already been to the cops.

MARTHA: Well?

KURT: They put together a statement with everything in it like it happened. I signed it. Today's Sunday, the people who got to look it over aren't there, but I'll be hearing from them. *(Nods)* The inspector who took my statement said there wasn't any need to lock me up. Or only later on, maybe. *(Looks at her. She is silent)* They sent a team out to the lake to check everything out and take samples of the water. And over to the clinic, because of Stefan. *(Pause)* And that's about it.

Pause.

SCENE FIVE

Martha in the kitchen. Evening. Kurt comes in from work.

KURT *(As he enters)*: First day. So far so good.

MARTHA: Anybody know about it at work yet?

KURT: I don't think so. Everything was just like always. The boss wasn't there all day.

MARTHA: I'll bet he's got plenty to keep him busy!

KURT: I'll say.

MARTHA *(Pause)*: Have a look in the bedroom.

KURT: Is he back?

MARTHA: See for yourself.

KURT *(Running into the bedroom, to the crib)*: Yeah. *(He smiles, takes Stefan out of the crib, cuddles him for a long time, weeping)*

SCENE SIX

In the garden patch. Lovely evening. Warm.

Martha and Kurt sitting on a little veranda. Stefan playing.

MARTHA: Isn't it beautiful?

KURT: Yep.

Pause. Martha suddenly begins to cry.

KURT: What's the matter?

MARTHA: Nothing. *(Pause)* I'm scared what's going to happen to us.

Short pause.

KURT: Go ahead, say what you were going to say.

MARTHA: If it gets around that you lied, and the boss finds out, that you didn't really have anybody backing you up, that'll be it for us, Kurt, don't you see that? He'll make sure you go to jail and he'll get an award for doing it. You can't get away with a lie for long.

KURT: It's not a lie anymore.

MARTHA: Why not?

KURT: I don't know what good it'll do, but the job steward

from the union knows, he came up to me yesterday
morning early just before pull-out and said he'd heard
something was going on.

MARTHA: Who from?

KURT: They got their channels.

MARTHA: But you're not even in the union!

KURT: 'Cause the boss always said he don't like it.

MARTHA: What did he want?

KURT: He said he'd got a tip, and if it was true what he
heard, what I told the police, they'd help us out. What
he said. *(Pause)* He said he'd come around on Saturday
afternoon and talk it over, him and some others.

MARTHA: What did you tell him?

KURT: I said, come on ahead.

MARTHA: What can they do?

KURT *(Uncertain, softly)*: Well, the union . . . that's a lot of
guys. *(Smiles a little)*

   Pause.

MARTHA: Look at Stefan, right in the middle of the flowers.

KURT: Leave him be . . .

NOTES

¹ A *Schrebgarten*: a unit of one of the municipally-owned garden plots grouped along rail lines and greenbelts, originally suggested by D.G.M. Schreber (1808-1861) as a healthy way for impecunious city-dwellers to get the advantages of fresh air and close contact with nature. *Schrebergarten* are still popular, and are often "willed" down generation after generation in families.

² Or, "By their fruits, you shall know them." Literally, "The crooked branch starts to curve early." So far as I know there is no equivalent proverb in English.

Mensch Meier

A Play of Everyday Life

This translation was made from the 1979 Suhrkamp edition of *Mensch Meier*. None of the original text is cut. A few lines, set off by square brackets, have been added where, in my opinion, cultural or political matters require clarification for an American audience.

On the Title: In colloquial German, "Mensch Meier" is an ejaculation of surprise, not necessarily pleasant. The exact (but out-of-date) English equivalent would be "Great Scott!" Since the German word "Mensch" means "human being," there's a flavor of universality about the title as well: "Meier-kind," on analogy with "mankind."

On Dialect: On this subject Kroetz says: "The characters speak Bavarian dialect. It would be better that they speak High German, though, than a dopey imitation 'dialect' that only makes them seem absurd." For an American production, any urban white working-class accent would be suitable, but the author's stricture applies: Unless the accents are effortless, genuine and consistent, it would be better to do entirely without. Particularly to be avoided is the notion that Germans speak stiffly, formally, without emotive intonation. For what it's worth, I "hear" Kroetz's characters speaking the unhasty, lilting, faintly querulous American of South Philadelphia. In the places where he is "role-playing," Otto speaks with a much more cultivated, i.e., TV-announcer, accent.

On the Setting: American producers may be tempted to adapt the piece to an American setting. In my opinion, this temptation is to be avoided. The basic action of the play revolves around Ludwig's unemployed status and his relationship with his father. To make the former correspond to North American mores and legalities regarding child labor, school-leaving age, etc., Ludwig would have to be 18 years old at the very least, which in turn would make his dependent relationship with his parents highly implausible. If, on the other hand, Ludwig's age is maintained at 15 or 16, the character becomes a "dropout," rather than the well-behaved, obedient son Kroetz has in mind. Either way, the principal motivating situation in the play is seriously compromised.

Martha, the wife, average, about 40 years old, a little hefty but not unattractive; very honest and practical.

Otto, the husband, also average and around 40, fairly big, lean, likes to smoke and drink, rather nervous, fidgety; in his best moments he comes across as almost elegant.

Ludwig [Ludi], the son, a nice kid of about 15; looks more like his father than his mother, growing up fast, but shy and sparing with his words; listening a lot, talking little.

[Cashier]

TIME

The spring and summer of 1976.

PLACE

Munich or nearby, perhaps in one of the high-rise housing projects built at Neuhausen around 1950.

Act One

SCENE ONE

Lazybones

The living room. The sofa bed is open. Ludwig is in it, but invisible; he has the covers pulled over his head. A faint sound of gentle, yearning English pop music comes from the bed. Around the bed, about three feet from it, is a little protective wall of personal treasures: a few cassettes, wallet, sunglasses, comb, a nice lighter, cigarettes, fairly fancy rocker-boots, jeans, short leather jacket, wristwatch, etc. Two or three posters on the walls.

MARTHA *(Calling from kitchen)*: Time to get up!

Ludwig doesn't respond.

Early bird gets the worm! *(Pause. She comes into the living room)* It's nearly eight and you're still lying in bed. Good grief, how many times do I have to call you? Get up now and don't waste the day God gave you.

LUDWIG *(Under the covers)*: Ten more minutes.

MARTHA: Not one minute more. Out I said, and straighten up. It's like a rat's nest in here. I want to clean.

LUDWIG *(Emerging)*: Why do I have to get up?

MARTHA: Because I say so. Imagine, [nearly sixteen and] still lying in bed when his poppa's been on the job an hour already. Look at you! Now get a move on before I lose my temper. *(She goes out again)* Nothing but trouble from morning till night.

Pause. Ludwig listens to the music a little longer, then switches it off. He puts the cassette recorder carefully aside, gets up and slowly gets dressed. Then he begins tidying the room. Since he does it daily, he has a routine: first he collects all his possessions in one place, then takes them to "his" drawer and stows everything in its place. Then he tidies further, takes the posters down from the wall (making sure no dirt comes with them), rolls them carefully together and puts them behind the dresser. Everything is clinically clean, only the bed remains. Then he leaves the room, we hear him enter the bathroom, turn on the water, etc.

Pause.

Martha comes busily in, goes to the sofa bed, shakes out the comforter and pillows, folds them and makes them into a bundle, opens the bed's storage space and puts them in it, folds the bed up into a proper living-room couch again. She straightens a few more things, puts a spread and a few cushions on the couch, tidies up and is satisfied that all traces of the night have vanished, that everything's tidy. She returns to the kitchen. Calling out:

Hurry up, the coffee won't stay warm forever!

LUDWIG *(From the bathroom)*: Coming!

SCENE TWO

Company

Saturday, mid-day; everybody is watching television in the living room.

LUDWIG: I saw somewhere [he's so dumb] he can't even write his own name. *(He laughs)*

MARTHA *(Angry)*: What kind of paper would say a thing like that? That man is a *king*!

OTTO: [They don't care what they say just so long as they're talking about "The Royal Wedding." That's all we had in the papers for a solid month.]

LUDWIG: [*Or* on TV.]

Pause.

OTTO: Just give me a tenth of the money he's got, I could get along just fine without writing my name.

MARTHA *(Nods)*: It's only people who are jealous say things like that anyway.

Pause.

OTTO: You think she's still a virgin? [Your magazines say anything about that?] I mean, a girl who's going to be a queen ought to be . . .

MARTHA *(Definitely)*: Of course not, at her age. Imagine, just an ordinary middle-class girl doing so well for herself.

LUDWIG: Who cares?

MARTHA: And a German girl at that! *(Nods)* "Germany's Golden Girl," even the King of Sweden couldn't resist her! *(Nods. Pause)* Our wedding was nice, too. *(Pause)* There, he said it: *(With pleasure)* Sylvia Renate Sommerlatt—imagine how she feels when she hears her name like that? *(Pause)* Now they've said "I do." *(Smiles and nods)* Now they exchange the rings.

OTTO: What do you think all this stuff cost, the whole
   circus?

MARTHA: Listen, she's whispering, so nobody else can hear
   her. *(Short pause. Firmly)* Very beautiful.

OTTO: She's got fat hands on her.

MARTHA: Don't be so silly. Oh, now they're going to sing.
   Men's voices are beautiful.

OTTO: Not these, they're not.

MARTHA: Well, they're only like cardinals, not real singers.
   We had a harmonium play at our wedding, remember?

Otto looks; he doesn't remember.

   What was it he played? "The Lovely Galatea" by Von
   Suppe! *(Nods)* You see, I remember and you don't.

OTTO: Sure.

Pause.

MARTHA: All the royalty and famous people in the world are
   there.

LUDWIG: Who *cares?*

MARTHA: Because you have no notion what's beautiful. . . .
   How many kings are there left in the world? You can
   count them on the fingers of one hand. A person ought
   to be thankful just to see it, an event like this.

OTTO *(Orotund)*: *Ep*-och-making. *(In his normal tone)* Course,
   they don't amount to anything anymore, your "crowned
   heads."

MARTHA: She's supposed to be very intelligent, Sylvia is.

OTTO: Not him, though. This one's got that right, anyway.
   (Referring to Ludwig) Just the same, you get to where he
   is and his money, then you can talk, not before.

MARTHA: Be quiet, this is where they become man and wife.
   (Laughs) She keeps peeking up at him, see?

OTTO *(Laughing)*: Poor SOB! She's got him now. "No, no,

you're not going nowhere, little fella," that's what she's thinking.

MARTHA *(Has to laugh)*: Oh, you men!

OTTO: Wham, the trap closes! *(Laughs, nods)*

Pause.

MARTHA: You hear that? "What is happiness? To forget yourself, and live for others."

OTTO: Easy for them to say.

MARTHA: What's beautiful about it and what I like, it's a real love-match. He saw her at the Olympics and said, "She's the one I want, whoever she is." That's the way a king ought to be!

Otto laughs.

LUDWIG: 'M hungry!

MARTHA: Wait till they're finished, can't you?

OTTO *(Looking at Ludwig, unemotional)*: I wouldn't mind having your life!

Ludwig just looks at him.

MARTHA: Everybody takes it easy on Saturday. Nearly everybody.

OTTO: Yeah? So what'd he do yesterday?

LUDWIG *(Looks at him, nervous)*: Nothing.

OTTO: Exactly. You could learn something from them there. *(Points at TV)* Te-le-vision!

MARTHA: So. That was nice. *(Emphatically)* Very, very nice. *(Nods. Pause)* Recognize them?

OTTO: Who?

MARTHA: The man doesn't see a thing! Queen Fabiola and King Bauduin! There's [our] President Scheel too and his wife.

OTTO: She looks like a hippo.

MARTHA *(Extenuatingly)*: Well, she's five-foot-eleven. . . .
   (Pause) Did you hear, she can speak six languages,
   Sylvia. Imagine! That's worth more than all the gold in
   China. . . . And the King has four sisters! Busy, busy!
OTTO *(Gives Ludwig a friendly punch)*: Get yourself one of
   them and you won't have nothing to worry about!

Ludwig shows his gratitude by laughing too hard.

MARTHA: Man proposes, God disposes. *(Means the wedding)*
   Now it's really over and they're going out of the church.
   Look at how they strut along. Imagine if you tripped,
   you'd wish you were dead! *(Laughs. Pause)* He's really
   nice, though, the King, look how he's always smiling!
   That's not easy.
OTTO: Sst! *(Points at screen. Pause)* The Reds don't like it.
   (Nods)
MARTHA: That's no way to act at a wedding, what's it got to
   do with politics, what it stands for.
OTTO: Sweden.
MARTHA: That's right.
LUDWIG: 'M hungry.
MARTHA: Listen to him talk, like he's the one who brings the
   money home to feed us. I want to watch the rest!
OTTO: Earn something, then you can give the orders. Right?
LUDWIG: OK.

   Pause.

MARTHA: The nicest thing about it, she's German.
OTTO: Suppose he married a black girl, what then?
MARTHA *(Fast, dismissive)*: Kings don't do things like that.
OTTO: Sure.

   Pause.

MARTHA: Everybody's standing up and cheering them! *(Short pause)* A real fairy tale wedding. *(Nods and smiles)*

LUDWIG *(Provoking her)*: Aren't we gonna eat at *all* today?

MARTHA *(Snapping back at him)*: Lazy loafers don't need to eat.

OTTO: I'm getting hungry too.

MARTHA *(Irritably)*: Ten more minutes! Men, they can't leave you in peace for a minute!

LUDWIG: Big deal.

OTTO *(Weakly complaining)*: Never going to amount to anything, always got to be out of step.

MARTHA: He's still young.

OTTO: Not much longer.

MARTHA: Young and silly.

They go back to watching. After a little Ludwig gets up, takes something out of "his" drawer and leaves. We hear a doorlatch snap shut. Otto and Martha don't notice.

Look at [the banner on] that housefront: "Juan Carlos, Murderer, Franco the Second."

OTTO: They shouldn't ought to allow that.

MARTHA: I hope *he* didn't notice. He's a king too, [just like Juan Carlos,] it could spoil the happiest day of his life.

OTTO: They didn't read it.

MARTHA: Well, I hope not, because it'd be a shame when they're so happy.

OTTO: You got to let people have their happiness.

MARTHA: Sylvia Sommerlatt, Queen of Sweden, from now on.

OTTO: 'M *hungry*.

MARTHA: Earn some money, you can go stuff yourself at Humpelmeyer's for all I care!

OTTO *(Thinks she's talking to him)*: What the hell way to talk
    is that?

MARTHA: What?

OTTO: That's what I ought to be asking!

MARTHA: Where did he go?

OTTO: Out somewhere.

MARTHA: Well, I'm going to watch it to the end and that's
    that! *(Pause)* White orchids for a bouquet! Look at how
    she keeps waving it around all the time, that's not right,
    somebody ought to tell her, people are sure to talk.

OTTO: They'll never know in Sweden.

MARTHA: Think so?

SCENE THREE

Coitus Interruptus

*In the bedroom: furniture from Neckermann's, nice. Otto and Martha
are going at it.*

MARTHA: What are you thinking about?

OTTO: Nothing.

   Pause. They do it.

MARTHA: You got something else on your mind.

OTTO: Hmmmh—!

MARTHA: No.

   Pause. They keep at it.

   I want to know what you're thinking about!

OTTO: What'd I say?

MARTHA: When you're in bed with me and thinking about
    something else, a person's got a right to put a stop to it.
    (She does) Completely inconsiderate!

OTTO: No, really, it's OK. No, hey . . .

MARTHA: What is it then? *(She has pulled free of him)*

OTTO: I didn't say anything . . .

MARTHA: Exactly.

OTTO: No, but. . . . It's embarrassing.

MARTHA: Well, thank you very much! The kind of things a woman has to put up with!

OTTO: No, you got the wrong idea. What it is, [this supervisor,] he borrowed my ballpoint, it must have been two weeks ago, it cost me twenty-eight seventy. *(Short pause)* And forgot to give it back. *(He turns over abruptly in bed. Pause)* I been thinking about it for a long time already, how I could lead up to asking for it back without getting him angry. Whether I should just go in and say "Excuse me, Chief, but you borrowed a ballpoint off me, please could I have it back?" Or maybe not "please," just "You think I could get it back?" Then he might just smile and say, "Sure, sorry about that." *(Laughs)* Then just reach in his pocket. . . . *(Short pause. Meaningfully)* If he still *got* it!

Pause. Martha hasn't really been listening, but since he's talking to her like a wife now she gradually manages to listen to him, but doesn't really understand the point yet since she was expecting something different.

What if he doesn't have it anymore? So he goes, "What did it look like?," and then I have to describe it, right? And then he looks around on his desk, and if he doesn't find it, then it could get embarrassing. "Are you sure it was me that borrowed it?" "Yes." "When was that?" "Oh, two weeks ago." "So why didn't you mention it before now?" *(Short pause)* What do I say then? *(Pause)*

What I'm afraid of. . . . *(Short pause)* What I think is, he didn't even hold onto it.

Nods, looks at Martha, who doesn't understand any of this.

He probably left it laying around the top floor somewhere that same day.

Long pause. Martha nods sympathetically.

It's hopeless.

Pause. He smiles and nods.

MARTHA *(Looking at him)*: Well, it's easy to do, I mean, a ballpoint, you just stick it in your pocket and don't think what you're doing.

OTTO *(Fast)*: Even if you see it cost something, it's worth something?

Martha looks at him.

Does the boss see things like that, that's the question, he probably takes expensive stuff for granted. You know? I even thought, what about I put a notice up on the bulletin board? "Lost ballpoint"—you know, diplomatic—"gunmetal gray, retractable point, red enamel cap, clearly marked, no Jap imitation: Pelikan Mercator Super model. Reward for return." *(Looks at his wife)* Five marks maybe. Since it cost twenty-eight. *(Looks at her)*

MARTHA: That won't help if the boss's got it.

OTTO: That's exactly my point, 'cause the boss don't have any reason to look at the bulletin board. And anybody else isn't going to give it back, not when they see what a nice piece of goods it is. He's going to stick it away and keep it for himself. *(Nods)* That's only human, it feels great in your hand and writes beautiful.

Long pause.

MARTHA *(Thinking about it)*: You should have gone right in and asked before he forgot about it.

OTTO *(Looks at her irritably)*: Listen to her! *(Pause)* He come in with a delegation, maybe twenty men, every one a section chief at least, most of them supervisors, brings them in personally, that was a special situation right there we thought, and he wanted to explain something and needed a ballpoint! *(He nods. Pause: a serious problem)* He asked me personally for it, which was kind of special too, explained the problem and then went on with the tour, *(Formally)* forgetting that he happens to have my pen. You think I'm going to stop them, the whole delegation, practically grab the boss by the elbow and make him give my pen back? *(Pause)* Impossible. *(Looks at his wife)*

MARTHA: Then you should have gone over to the office as soon as they were finished.

OTTO: As soon as they were finished they all went over to the Casino for a banquet to celebrate getting a thirty million-mark contract. *(Emphatically)* Impossible.

MARTHA: What about the next day?

OTTO: He was in Brussels.

MARTHA: How do you know?

OTTO *(Quietly)*: Because I am not stupid and was planning to go over and checked beforehand to find out if he was there. Negative.

Pause.

MARTHA: So why didn't you do it the day after?

Pause.

OTTO: I didn't have the nerve.

MARTHA *(Sniffs)*: Well, for pity's sake, if at first you don't succeed, you know what they say.

OTTO: Well, it was too late then.

Pause.

MARTHA: Then there's nothing to do, it's just bad luck.

OTTO: Yep. I'll just have to forget my Mercator. *(Pause)* But catch me buying another one that expensive. The cheap ones write good enough and you don't have to worry about them.

MARTHA *(Laughs)*: You go ahead and buy another good one!

Otto laughs, pleasantly surprised.

But if the boss or someone comes around again, you just put it away quick, or always have a cheap one in your pocket you can give him if you have to.

OTTO: If I got another Mercator I wouldn't even take it to work, I'd keep it at home where nothing can happen to it.

MARTHA *(Nodding)*: Let things out of your sight and they're gone. . . .

OTTO: But you got to admit I take care of my stuff, don't I? It's been a long time since I've lost anything. I've had that gold cigarette lighter six years.

MARTHA: Well, but what about that silver money clip I gave you, I haven't seen it for a long time?

OTTO: 'Cause I don't carry it, 'cause it's broken, and anyway it's not my style. But I got it right in the night table, I could reach it from here.

MARTHA: That's all right, then.

OTTO: I still got everything I ever had that's worth something.

Pause.

MARTHA *(Nods)*: And there's no way you could know the
boss was going to walk up and borrow your ballpoint.
OTTO: I had a funny feeling as soon as he said, "Do you
happen to have something to write with?" and boom, it's
gone.

Pause.

MARTHA *(With a sidelong look at him)*: Go to sleep now and
forget about it. *(Pause)* Sleep tight.
OTTO: Thanks, you too. And I'll forget about the ballpoint.
MARTHA: That's right.

SCENE FOUR

World Champion

*Otto sits in a very, very small room. No window. It seems to be a closet of
sorts which Otto has turned into a hobby room. He's working on a model
plane, which is complicated by the fact that the plane's wingspan (between
two and four meters, after all!) makes it hard to deal with. After
working for a long time, he suddenly begins to speak [with a TV-
announcer accent].*

OTTO: I know it's not customary to disturb a contestant just
before a race, *(Artificial laugh)* but Otto, if you could just
take time to answer a few questions for our viewers.
—Sure, go ahead! —Your career in sports could be
called nothing short of meteoric. You began participating
actively in model airplane competition just two years
ago, and in that time astonishing as it seems you've taken
the national championships for both short- and middle-
distances. And now you're on the trail of the European
Title as a stepping stone, so to speak, to the

Championship of the World. Will you win today? *(He
gives the fake laugh again)* When you think of all the titles
you've pulled down in just the last few months already, it
wouldn't surprise our audience too much if you did it
again today. How does a man learn to fly like that?
—Well, I think you've got to have an understanding of
how the atmosphere works to start with, and a real love
of flying, and of course a lot of luck.

—How long have you been flying model planes? —I
started fifteen years ago, if you go back all the way to
the beginning. But of course the techniques were
completely different back then.

—Let me break in here for just one question: You fly
only models you've built with your own hands? —Yes.
—The experts tell me that's another big reason for your
success. One writer for a model magazine called it, and I
quote, "a kind of genius for aero-engineering." Do you
agree? —Well, you shouldn't blow your own horn, but of
course you got to have some natural ability, because
models you see are all pretty much state-of-the-art
already. And the big manufacturers have a lot of
advantages. Like I don't have my own wind tunnel, for
example.

—And you used to be, you don't mind my asking this
I'm sure, a worker on an assembly line? —Yes, I was.
—But today the hobby has grown into a full-time
occupation, what with your model airplane factory and
all. —You could put it that way.

—Mr. Meier, all of us and I'm sure all our viewers at
home wish you the very best of luck in the European
Title trials here in Rome, and hope that the name of the
next holder of the European Long-Distance Model
Airplane Championship will be Otto Meier of Germany.

Thank you! —And now ladies and gentlemen we return you to ZDF Sports Central.

He sniffs. He looks up a little and almost looks around to see if he's been overheard. Then, still "in character," he labors grimly away at the greatest model airplane in the world.

SCENE FIVE

Next Stop: Freedom

In a department store. Otto is trying on a "leisure suit." Martha is considering the result.

MARTHA: I don't know. *(Shakes her head; she doesn't like it)*
OTTO: Me neither.
MARTHA *(Nodding)*: It looks kind of cheap.
OTTO: Well, it *is* cheap.
MARTHA: Exactly. The other one is better.
OTTO: It ought to, it costs enough.
MARTHA: But this one really does look cheap.
OTTO: You shouldn't be able to tell just by looking that I'm some guy off the line with a couple weeks' vacation coming.
MARTHA: That's just what this looks like! The other one's more *(Smiling)* I don't know . . . international.
OTTO: Man of leisure. *(Laughs)*
MARTHA: Because it really is a leisure suit. In this one anybody can see you don't get much time off. Not so much with the other one; it's more . . . casual.
OTTO: Because it costs almost twice as much.
MARTHA: Quality has its price. *(Short pause)* Get the other one. *(Nods)*

SCENE SIX

Happiness

*Otto and Martha at home in the little kitchen eating dinner. Otto
laughs; eats; looks to see if Martha has reacted to his laugh. She hasn't.
Pause. Otto takes something out of his pocket.*

OTTO: Know what that is?

MARTHA *(Looks)*: It's a ballpoint, what about it?

OTTO *(Shaking his head)*: Some memory you got! It's my
    Pelikan Mercator Super; the same one! *(Laughs)*

MARTHA: The one you lost?

OTTO: What else? There she is. Ta-dah!

MARTHA *(Looking)*: There, and you were so sure it
    was gone for good.

OTTO: Like we talked, I decided to forget all about it, you
    know? *(Laughs)* But I put up a notice on the bulletin
    board anyway.

MARTHA: And the boss saw it?

OTTO: No, course not, it was just like we thought: he left it
    lying around somewhere and someone else picked it up.

MARTHA: And gave it back?

OTTO *(Nods)*: And you know who it was? *(Looks)* One of
    them I would have sworn on the Bible would never give
    it back.

MARTHA: You can't tell a book by its cover.[1]

OTTO *(Laughs)*: How's that for luck?

SCENE SEVEN

Life

In a beer garden. Otto, Martha and Ludwig. Beautiful warm day.

OTTO: You got to take the time sometimes just to enjoy life.

MARTHA: Beautiful Sunday weather. It was a good idea
coming out here.

OTTO: Looks like the lord and master's enjoying himself too.

LUDWIG: 'S that mean I can have another beer?

OTTO: Request granted. *(Laughs)*

LUDWIG: A stein this time!

OTTO: A glass is all. Don't get big ideas.

SCENE EIGHT

Pipedreams

Morning in the kitchen. Martha and Ludwig.

MARTHA: Look at him sit there the whole morning like he
hasn't got a thing to do.

LUDWIG: What am I supposed to do?

MARTHA: Decent people always have something to do.

LUDWIG: You want me to go shopping for you?

MARTHA: That's my job.

Pause.

LUDWIG: At the employment office they said they'd let me
know when I was supposed to come in again. Anyway, I
was there last week and I'm going in next week whether
they call me or not.

MARTHA: You have to stay on the ball.

LUDWIG: Oh sure. But if you go in too often without them

asking then the counselor gets mad at you, I already noticed that, then I *really* won't get anything.

MARTHA: Other boys have jobs already, only you.

LUDWIG: Well, what do you want me to do, Momma, tell me.

MARTHA: What do I know about it, I don't know anything. You have to be up and doing, show some initiative, that's what you have to do. Look around. Keep your ears open for where they need people.

LUDWIG: I ought to just go down to the post office and get the business directory and call up all the big companies [and say, "Hello, this is Ludwig Meier, I got a seventy-eight in my school finals, send a limo round for me right away."]

MARTHA: [Fine way to talk, young man.] Frittering good money away on the telephone.

LUDWIG: Well? [What then?]

Pause.

MARTHA: To get along in this world you have to play by the rules.

LUDWIG: No.

MARTHA *(Quickly)*: Don't talk that way!

Ludwig grins and nods.

You're a good boy. But with you sitting around like this all the time, it makes me nervous and I just get furious.

LUDWIG: But I don't know what to do, Momma. *(Short pause)* I can't just go sit on a bench like the old people. *(Pause. He looks at her and laughs)* If you want I can hang myself, then I'll *really* be out of the way. . . .

MARTHA: You could do that to your parents, that's the thanks we get! *(Pause. Firmly, stubbornly)* Dental technician, loan officer, tax agent. *(Pause)* Shine your poppa's shoes, there's a good boy, it makes him happy to see that you want to do the right thing, then he won't be after you all night when he gets home.

Ludwig goes into the entry hall and gets to work polishing shoes. Pause.

LUDWIG: Anyway, it doesn't matter how you make your money just as long as you have some.

MARTHA *(From the kitchen)*: What?

LUDWIG: I said it doesn't matter how you make your money, just so long as it's an honest job.

MARTHA: That's enough of that.

Pause.

LUDWIG: But if you and Poppa think I'm going to get a good apprenticeship like what you're talking about, that's not going to happen. You're just dreaming.

MARTHA *(Loudly)*: We are no such thing. You have a right to job training, that's the law, that's why we pay our taxes to the government, so our son doesn't have to be a common laborer.

LUDWIG: I'm not talking about common labor. But bricklayer . . .

MARTHA *(Quickly)*: You think bricklayers are happy?

LUDWIG: What?

MARTHA: Look at your father, that's no way to live.

LUDWIG: He's not a bricklayer . . .

MARTHA: It's the same thing, a laborer is a laborer.

LUDWIG: Well, so? If there weren't any laborers . . .

MARTHA: Now that's enough, I said. I'd like to know where you got this nonsense, not around here, that's for sure. *(Pause)* It's as plain as the nose on your face. They'll take anybody as a laborer, [look at the kind of people you

see working on those jobs,] it doesn't take anything
special.

LUDWIG: But they're taking apprentices in the building
trades, they told me at the employment office.

MARTHA: Oh, I can believe that, because they can't find
enough [German] boys dumb enough to take jobs like
that. You have to get ahead in life. Even in a family
[from one generation to the next]. Your poppa is [just] a
laborer, never mind the money's not bad. It's too late to
change that. But you *(Formal)* have to climb the next
rung of the ladder, otherwise nothing we've done for you
makes any sense.

Ludwig is silent. Martha comes to him in the hall.

You'll see, when you have a son of your own . . .

LUDWIG: He's going to have to be president, at least.

MARTHA: Idiot. *(Pause)* Time is fleeting.

LUDWIG: I know it. In July more kids will be getting out of
school and they'll need jobs too and some of them are
going to have better diplomas than I do.

MARTHA: Because you didn't study hard enough. There's
nothing wrong with your brains, no one can tell me that.

LUDWIG: I passed my exams.

MARTHA: By the skin of your teeth.

LUDWIG: Other guys didn't.

MARTHA: All right, and that's why you're going to be a
dental technician and not a bricklayer.

LUDWIG: Keep dreaming, Momma.

MARTHA: Don't be smart when someone only wants what's
best for you.

LUDWIG: I've been sitting around for eight months . . .

MARTHA *(Furiously)*: You talk like it's our fault you're out of
work!

LUDWIG: If I'd apprenticed as a bricklayer right away I'd almost be in my second year now.

MARTHA: And someone asks, "What's your son doing now?" —"Oh, he's a bricklayer's helper . . ."

LUDWIG: What's the matter with that?

MARTHA: . . . [As if you were no better than some of these foreigners!] That's what I'd have to tell them. I'd rather say . . .

LUDWIG: "My son? Oh, he's dead."

MARTHA: That's an awful thing to say. *(Pause)* You don't have the slightest understanding of what your parents want for you. That's what it is.

LUDWIG: You don't understand either.

MARTHA: He can say that, sit there and do nothing and just let himself slide.

LUDWIG: Right, because around here everybody's living in a dream world, that's why!

MARTHA: We've been too good to you. If we got strict with you, then you'd see soon enough. *(Pause)* It's easy enough to say, "Go on, earn some money. Go into the factory or into construction or where you like, just bring something home." But honey, you mustn't get used to living like that, or you'll never get away. *(Pause)* You're all we've got, if I could only make you understand.

Ludwig looks at her.

SCENE NINE

Recollections

At dinner in the kitchen. Martha and Otto.

OTTO: You know, I just about decided I been screwed.

MARTHA: When?

OTTO: Last week when we went to the Löwenbräukeller, don't you remember?

MARTHA: Of course I do, it was beautiful.

OTTO: I paid sixty-six marks twenty including tip; call it sixty-seven marks.

MARTHA: That's a lot, but it was really nice.

OTTO: Monday I was standing on the line and was thinking back about what a good weekend it was, and you know what hit me?

MARTHA: Nothing sensible, I'm sure.

OTTO: I suddenly realized the waiter must have screwed me, because what we had, that couldn't have cost any sixty-six twenty.

MARTHA: Really, even with the pickled pork?

OTTO: Twenty-six marks.

MARTHA: That's a lot, but when you think how all three of us picked it over, it looked like more than there was, but we all got some.

OTTO: It was pretty dry, just the same.

MARTHA: Then you had three beers.

OTTO: Four twenty each, already figured in: twelve sixty.

MARTHA: And I had . . . [*(Trying to recall)*]

OTTO: I remember if you don't. You had two glasses of wine and an ale before that.

MARTHA: I forgot all about the ale.

OTTO: But I didn't. The wine cost nine twenty-five. And there's something funny about that too; how can two times anything come out with a five on the end?

MARTHA: The waiter must have made a mistake.

OTTO: How?

MARTHA: It couldn't amount to much anyway, because I remember I didn't want the Bernkastler, even at three sixty, and then there were only two others on the menu and one was too expensive, over five marks a glass it was . . .

OTTO: Ridiculous.

MARTHA: . . . so there was only the one in between, that was the May wine, and it was four marks . . . four fifty, I think.

OTTO: All right, so that doesn't matter. Twenty-six for the pork, three beers twelve sixty, plus wine . . .

MARTHA: And the ale.

OTTO: How much was that?

MARTHA: I don't know.

OTTO: Why not?

MARTHA: Well, for goodness' sake, you don't look at the price before you order a glass of ale, do you?

OTTO: I know what everything I ordered for me and the kid cost, because I studied the menu, the prices, before I ordered. *(Pause)* Over to the Ratskeller they charge one sixty for a glass of ale.

Martha stares at him.

Just for comparison. Call it another mark, because the Löwenbräukeller is so well-known and popular.

Martha nods.

Thirty-eight sixty plus two seventy is forty-one thirty, plus the wine, nine *(With emphasis)* twenty-five, that comes to fifty fifty-five.

MARTHA: Fifty marks.

OTTO: No, let's do this right. Ludi had a half-glass of wine to start with and then a glass of beer . . .

MARTHA: He wanted a stein, remember?

OTTO: Let him earn his own money and he can have a gallon as far as I'm concerned. I never got beer at all

when I was his age. Now we're getting down to it,
because I know for a fact that Ludi's wine cost two
ninety and the beer was two thirty. That's interesting; a
stein costs four twenty and it's twice as big, so anybody
who orders a glass is paying a penalty.

MARTHA: Oh, for goodness' sake . . .

OTTO: All right, let's total up. Fifty fifty-five plus two
ninety is fifty-three forty-five and two thirty is fifty-five
seventy-five. *(Pause)* And that's the problem; where did
the other ten marks go? Funny business? Maybe the
waiter made a little mistake on purpose when he was
adding up the bill. That could be what happened. It
makes me so mad I can't tell you. I haven't been able to
enjoy anything since.

MARTHA: Well, that's not a very nice thing to do, screw
someone out of ten marks.

OTTO: It sure isn't, if. . . . Oh, boy! *(Laughs. Pause)* I'll give
you a hint. Pretzels![2] Off the menu!

MARTHA: Well, of course!

OTTO *(Nods)*: That's what it was. We even had a big
discussion about it, remember? The pretzel girl came to
the table with those big pretzels, and we got three,
because everybody wanted one, and it was right before
we were going to leave, too. And I was going to pay for
them with a hundred, and the pretzel girl said she
couldn't change a hundred, pay her later when she had
change. And then she didn't come back. And then when
I was paying the waiter I told him, "Wait a minute, we
had three of those big pretzels too and we didn't pay the
girl for them yet, let me pay you and you settle up with
her. . . ."

MARTHA: Do you suppose he did?

OTTO: Would he cheat someone he works with? That's the

missing ten fifty, all right. Three fifty each. It all comes
out even. *(Pause)* When I thought of the pretzels, it was
like a weight falling off me.

MARTHA: When you get cheated it makes you feel that way.

OTTO: But it's all right now. *(Pause)* We got to the bottom of
it. *(Nods; he is exhausted)* I'm really tired.

MARTHA: Well, it's late.

SCENE TEN

Going for the Top

*Otto alone on a little hill. He's wearing the leisure suit. He has a gadget
in his hand and is staring up into the sky at his toy plane.*

OTTO: There's no place for fear in this business. *(Laughs)* Of
course, it's not easy to get life insurance when you're a
test pilot, but *(Laughs, shrugs)* you can die just as easily
in bed. *(Pause)* Jesus, if anybody heard me. . . . *(Looks
around, sees no one, smiles)* And when you're up there . . .
you're free! *(Laughs, nods)*

Act Two

SCENE ONE

Shadowplay

It is evening in the little apartment kitchen. Otto is nursing a beer—it must be after dinner—and staring into space, smoking. Ludwig is reading an auto magazine. Martha laboriously repairs Ludwig's leather jacket. Pause. Otto looks around, almost says something but suppresses it. Pause.

OTTO: What are you doing there, *(Emphatically formal)* so late in the night and all?

MARTHA: You can see perfectly well what I'm doing.

OTTO: You should let him fix his own trash, he's got plenty of time.

MARTHA *(Calm, but you can tell something's up)*: Leather is harder to fix than anything else. He can't do it.

OTTO: And I'm going around with holes in my socks.

MARTHA *(Looks at him angrily)*: What's that?

Otto doesn't answer.

What's eating you? Hmm? And why are you taking it out on us?

OTTO: Nothing.

MARTHA: Then just be quiet.

OTTO: He's got money for that junk, anyway. *(Meaning Ludwig's magazine)*

MARTHA: He can buy whatever he wants with his allowance.

Ludwig is about to say something, decides not to.

OTTO: As long as I earn it for him, he can. *(Short pause)* Does the young gentleman have any prospects for employment?

Ludwig shakes his head. Otto laughs.

Everybody in the world has to work, while young Mister Meier sits there and reads his magazine. Pretty soft situation, I'd say.

MARTHA: Leave him alone!

OTTO: Always defending our little prince.

Pause. Ludwig gets a packet of cigarettes out of his shirt-pocket and lights up; he's nervous.

Yes sir, he's going to end up just fine.

Pause.

MARTHA: Otto, what's bothering you? *(Pause)* Otto?

OTTO: Silly question, nothing. Just looking at him sitting there drives me up the wall.

LUDWIG: If you give me fifty marks for the rock festival, you wouldn't have to look at me for three days.

OTTO: Earn some money, then you can go to Paris if you feel like it.

Martha watches, keeps on with her mending.

LUDWIG: As an advance on my allowance!

OTTO: An advance on his allowance, listen to your little prince. That's rich. He acts like he was hired to waste

his time and do nothing around here, so naturally he
wants an advance on his pay.

LUDWIG: Then forget it.

Pause.

MARTHA: I can't give it to him out of the household budget.
But if he was away over the holiday you wouldn't have to
look at him and it might be better. Out of sight, out of
mind.

OTTO: I never got something for nothing in my life.

MARTHA: Who ever said you did?

OTTO: Kuno Gruschke lost his job.

MARTHA: What?

OTTO: Forty-seven men laid off. Fourteen Italians, eight
Turks, the Iranian, fifteen women and nine *(Formal)*
"senior employees." Kuno was one of them.

MARTHA *(Looking at him)*: Be glad it wasn't you.

OTTO: Yeah, well what if he was my friend? Just about the
only one.

MARTHA: It's too bad.

OTTO: Everything just keeps rolling along just the same as if
he never been there. Just gone. Nothing slowed down, no
problems. "Redisposition of Resources." I've got two
more screws to put in, a couple of other guys too. Up
ahead there's a kid does the door handle, he's new. Five
of the nine were off my line. From farther up, don't even
know what they did. The foreman was already there with
the new breakdowns. Five men, just like the earth
opened up and swallowed them.

MARTHA: You have to go along with the way things are.
They're picking out the older ones. You're not one of
them.

OTTO: You're right there, forty-two's not old.

MARTHA: The best years of your life.

OTTO: If only it hadn't of been Kuno. The union council went along with it. "It's in the contract." "You can't argue with facts." Cutting out the fat, they call it. "You have to stay flexible to keep up with the times." The way things are you can forget about finding a job when you're fifty-eight. *(Softly)* "Early retirement!"

MARTHA: He'll have time to enjoy life.

OTTO *(Loud)*: He doesn't want to enjoy life, he wants to work! *(Points at Ludwig; softly)* Will you look at him there?

MARTHA: This is no reason to bully him. This isn't the first time people have been laid off. You never got worked up like this before.

OTTO: It's like an epidemic. First twenty-five, then thirty-one, another thirty-one, now forty-seven. When they get to forty-eight, it's mass layoffs, that's in the contract.

MARTHA: What does that mean?

OTTO: It means they can't pretty it up anymore, they're running out of time and got to do something fast. It means that this isn't the end, it's just the beginning. *(Pause)* I don't have anything to worry about, these are my best years, I'm good at my job. Some of the men tried to argue, they turned down the new plan to work around the vacancies. The foreman just looked at them. I knew what he felt like saying.

MARTHA: What about you?

OTTO: I said fine, sure, swell, nothing to it, and he slapped me on the shoulder and said, "Good for you!" I know what that means, too. *(Short pause)* It means security, thank God. *(He is perspiring)*

MARTHA: Is it easy to do the extra work?

OTTO: I got to screw down the housing for the left wing-

window, put in one more Gruschke used to do.
Somebody sixty feet back had the wing-window, I never
knew him. *(Nods)* Everything's split up different. *(Pause)*
They slow the line down a couple days till you got the
new moves into your hands. Then it's rolling again,
(Sniffs) and when it speeds up you got to stay on top of
it and not let your mind wander, like the foreman says.

MARTHA: If you do your best, it'll be all right.

*Otto nods, sweating as if after heavy labor; sniffs, smokes, sips his
beer. Pause. Ludwig looks at his father.*

OTTO: What are you looking at?

LUDWIG: Nothing. *(He reads on, that is to say buries his nose in
the magazine)*

OTTO: Good thing. You're not going to be around here to
look at me much longer, anyway. You can go find
yourself somebody else to stare at.

LUDWIG: Can I have the fifty marks?

OTTO: No.

Ludwig looks at him. Pause.

SCENE TWO

Worldly Wisdom

[Otto and Ludwig.] Saturday morning, the hallway. With shoes.

OTTO: When you got as much time as you got, you can get
it perfect.

LUDWIG: Uh-huh.

OTTO: You make yourself useful, nobody notices you. Look
here, *(Takes a shoe)* in between the sole and the leather,

that's the critical point, you can't get in there with the brush, you don't even touch the dirt, so it builds up.

LUDWIG: Uh-huh.

OTTO: Now here's the trick. *(Takes a piece of cord out of his pocket)* You take care of the problem with this. *(Laughs)* You get in there and clean right down to the bottom.

Otto takes the shoe between his knees, holds it there, and scours with the cord, which he holds in both hands and tugs rapidly back and forth in the recalcitrant crack between sole and upper. Ludwig watches. Holding up the string:

The proof! Look how much darker it is, see the dirt?

LUDWIG: Uh-huh.

OTTO: OK, you try it.

Ludwig looks at him.

You ought to be glad, somebody shows you how to do something.

Ludwig imitates his movements and cleans a shoe.

When you're finished call me, I'll inspect it.

LUDWIG: OK.

OTTO: You can come out flying this afternoon.

LUDWIG: I was planning to do something else.

OTTO: What's that?

Ludwig looks at him, doesn't answer.

Well, that's nice, a person offers to take you along to break in the new model. A test flight.

LUDWIG: I don't care about your old test flight.

OTTO: Well, I do. I care a lot about it.

LUDWIG: I know.

OTTO: The conquest of nature.

LUDWIG: I know.

OTTO: When you're not up there, when you're on the ground steering, it's harder than if you were sitting right in the plane. That's what the experts say. *(Pause)* It's the eye that does it, you got to be able to read the wind. *(Laughs)*

Ludwig nods.

You'll never get the hang of it, flying. *(Looks at Ludwig a while, then goes into the kitchen)*

MARTHA: Let's go shopping now, it's Saturday and the store's going to be crowded if we don't hurry.

LUDWIG: Bring me a pack of cigarettes back?

MARTHA: Sure. That's your pay.

Ludwig polishes shoes. Otto and Martha put their coats on and go out.

SCENE THREE

Market Crash

At the checkstand of a supermarket. Martha and Otto have made a fairly large purchase; both, especially Otto, are peeking into the market baskets of other customers in the checkout line.

OTTO *(To Martha, softly)*: Look.

MARTHA: What?

OTTO: Them up there.

Otto indicates with a guilty tilt of the head. Martha looks.

Look what they got in that basket.

Martha nods ["So what?"]

With tomorrow Sunday! Two packages of soup mix, a

pickle, two bottles of beer and a loaf of bread.
Understand? That's for a whole family, those two kids
are with them.

MARTHA: Maybe they did most of their shopping yesterday
and just forgot a few things.

OTTO: Fat chance! Two packages of Maggi, a pickle, bread
and two bottles of beer? *(Nods, laughs knowingly)* He's
out of work, that's what it is.

MARTHA: How can you tell?

OTTO: You got eyes in your head you can tell.

Both look.

MARTHA: Our turn!

*Martha unloads the groceries onto the little conveyor belt of the
checkstand while the cashier totals them and puts them into another
cart.*

CASHIER: Seventy-three ninety-four.

Martha is poking around in her purse.

Seventy-three ninety-four.

MARTHA *(Nods, blushing furiously; to Otto)*: Do you have any
money? I don't have enough.

*Otto goes red too, looks around at the people watching. He speaks
loudly, to shift the embarrassment off himself.*

OTTO: It's not my problem you come out without money!

MARTHA: I had a hundred marks in here and now there's
only fifty!

CASHIER: What's the problem? It comes to seventy-three
marks ninety-four pfennig [pronounced "fennig"].

MARTHA *(In total confusion)*: We'll have to put back
everything that comes to more than fifty-four marks.

CASHIER: But I already rung it up!

MARTHA: I'm sorry.

OTTO *(Audibly)*: Will you look what I married. Let me through, miss, *(To the Cashier)* this has nothing to do with me, she gets eight-hundred fifty a month for housekeeping.

MARTHA: Be quiet!

Otto pushes past the checkstand and runs out. To the Cashier:

I'm Mrs. Meier, you certainly must know me by now, don't you?

SCENE FOUR

Nightwatch

In the kitchen. Martha is crying. Otto stares at his son.

OTTO: You're going to pay for this.

Martha looks up. Otto nods.

MARTHA: Think how humiliated we were. It was horrible.

OTTO *(Nods)*: You do a thing like that to your parents.

Otto gives Ludwig a clout on the head. Ludwig takes it, stares straight ahead, doesn't react.

(Unmoved) I want an answer. Where did you hide the fifty marks you stole?

Ludwig stares, says nothing.

MARTHA: Give it back, you've got to give it back when you steal something or it only makes it worse.

Ludwig stares.

OTTO: And this is supposed to be my son, now I've got a better idea what my son is.

No reaction from Ludwig.

Next we'll have my son the convicted criminal. *(Otto jumps up, runs into the living room, goes to the sofa bed where Ludwig sleeps, yanks it open and tears the bedclothes apart. He finds nothing, comes back)* Give me the fifty marks or there's going to be trouble.

MARTHA: Otto!

OTTO: You know what your son is? He's an animal. *(Nods)* That's why nobody will hire him, they could see it even if we couldn't. Personnel managers are trained, they see it right away: this young man is a thief! I'm going to count to three, now, and when I'm finished the fifty marks better be on the table. One. Two. Three.

Otto looks at Ludwig. Ludwig doesn't react. Otto jumps up again and runs back into the living room, pulls out Ludwig's drawer, throws everything out of it, rummages through it, tears up the posters; looks, finds nothing, comes back, looks at his son.

MARTHA: Give the fifty marks back, Ludi, don't push Poppa too far.

OTTO: You hear what your Momma said? He doesn't hear. He's tough. You're not tough enough for me. I'm going to finish you off once and for all if that's what it takes.

Otto and Ludwig stare at each other. No reaction from Ludwig.

Down with your pants.

Ludwig looks at him.

Put the money on the table, wherever you've got it.

Ludwig looks at him.

Down with your pants, I said. You want me to help you?

Pause. At first Ludwig doesn't react, then he removes his jeans. Otto grabs them and rifles them, finds nothing.

Keep going.

Ludwig looks at him, then pulls off his leather jacket. Otto searches it, finds nothing. Ludwig looks at him.

(Wildly) Give me the fifty marks, don't push me too far, I warn you. *(Screaming)* Give me my fifty marks!

Ludwig stares.

Where did you hide it, just tell me.

Ludwig remains silent.

The rest of the clothes, come on, quickly, that's an order.

Ludwig abruptly begins crying uncontrollably. The tears run down his cheeks as he takes off the rest of his clothes garment by garment until he is naked. Otto stares at him, frozen; there's no trace of the fifty marks. Long pause.

(Suddenly light, forgiving) There's no need to be ashamed in front of your parents, we saw you when you were a little boy. *(Nods)*

Pause. Martha turns her face away, she doesn't want to see Ludwig naked.

You're proud, aren't you? Because you're sly, you won't give the secret away. *(Nods)* I can see that. *(Short pause)* You'll never amount to anything, I guarantee you, you can count on it. I know the way the world is, it hasn't got any use for your kind, as sure as God made Adam. You're not our kind at all.

LUDWIG *(Looking at his father, quiet, still crying)*: I'd rather be dead than be like you.

Otto's control almost snaps. He looks at his son.

OTTO *(To Martha)*: You hear that?

MARTHA *(Still crying)*: What?

Long pause.

OTTO: That's how I feel. Just the same.

Otto looks at Ludwig one more time, then suddenly oblivious of the others, goes uncertainly into his workroom. Long pause.

MARTHA: Put something on, you'll catch cold.

Ludwig gathers his things up quickly, goes into the living room and gets dressed there.

(To herself) It's not so terrible, there are a lot worse things. *(Nods some spirit back into herself)*

Ludwig has gotten dressed; now he puts his things away, sorrowing over the torn posters, etc. Then he gets a suitcase, packs what he needs and wants to take with him into it, gets his toilet articles out of the bathroom. When he's packed he comes back into the kitchen. Martha watches. Ludwig reaches under a stack of saucers in the kitchen cabinet and takes out the fifty marks.

(Watching) Take care of yourself and don't get into trouble. Come back soon.

Ludwig nods, sticks the money in his pocket and leaves the apartment. Martha watches him go. A very long pause. Otto comes out of his workroom into the kitchen.

OTTO: He gone?

Martha nods. Pause. Otto sits down on the left side of the table, looks at Martha. Long pause.

MARTHA *(Very calmly)*: Otto, I'll never forgive you for this.
OTTO *(Looks at her)*: Why?

Long pause.

SCENE FIVE
Count Down[3]

Otto and Martha are watching television late at night in the living room.

Otto drinks a sip of beer.

Martha looks accusingly at him.

Otto does not react.

Pause. They watch television.

Otto pours out more beer, drinks.

Pause.

Martha gets up, goes into the kitchen, looks to see if she has taken the chicken off the stove, waits in the kitchen, comes back, sits down again.

Pause.

Martha looks at Otto.

Otto drinks some more beer.

The TV plays on. It is a Western. Pause.

Otto pours more beer, dropping a little inadvertently on the carpet.

Martha notices, jumps up, runs into the kitchen, gets a towel, dampens it with hot water from the water heater by the sink, runs back into the living room, kneels down and virtuously wipes up the spot.

Otto is disturbed, has to move his feet out of the way.

Martha gives him a reproachful look and wipes away.

Otto watches Martha as she cleans by his feet, then takes the bottle and deliberately shakes a tiny drop onto the rug beside his wife where she kneels at his feet.

Martha notices, but only stares at Otto.

Otto puts the beer bottle down again.

Martha sniffs with careful audibility, then cleans up the new spot with ceremonious fussiness.

Otto drinks off the last of his glass, watching.

Martha looks him reproachfully right in the eye, then goes on cleaning.

Otto watches, sniffs, starts to pour another glass.

Martha looks at him accusingly.

Otto smashes the bottle on the living-room table without warning.

Martha jumps up, screams.

Otto gets up.

Martha thinks she's in danger, screams even louder.

Otto goes to the TV set and wipes it off the buffet with one shove.

Martha stares, too scared now to scream.

Otto destroys everything that comes to hand, smashing vases on the wall, overturning furniture, throwing chairs against the wall, pulling up the carpet; this goes on for a long time.

Martha runs from one corner to the other to avoid being hurt.

Otto runs into his workshop and smashes everything to pieces, takes an almost finished model and gives it special treatment, throwing it several times against the wall until it is in fragments; then he starts for the kitchen.

Martha leaps to meet him like a Fury incarnate, stands in the kitchen door, ready for anything.

MARTHA: You come in here over my dead body, you understand me?

Otto looks at his wife, then turns away, stands a little while like a passenger at a train station waiting for his connection, looks around, sees the mess he's made. Suddenly a tremor goes through him; he flings himself with all the force in him at the wall, bangs his head against it as hard as he can; he yowls, but does it again, trying to smash through the wall with his head.

Pause.

Otto suddenly goes into the bathroom and washes his hands very thoroughly with soap. He stares into the mirror.

(Fast) A broken mirror's seven years' bad luck, that's what they say. *(Nods)*

Otto looks at himself attentively in the mirror. Pause.

SCENE SIX

Silence

The next day, Sunday, Martha and Otto. A very long, painful scene. It consists of the two bringing "order" back to things. Otto tries to save what can be saved (tries to fix a chair, etc.) while Martha mainly cleans. This goes on for a long time.

SCENE SEVEN

On the Moon

It is evening. Otto and Martha are sitting in the living room, brought back to some semblance of order. Pause.

MARTHA: That's all we needed. *(Nods)* If the picture tube is cracked, you can just throw the whole set right out. I figure the damage amounts to a thousand marks at least—*(Emphatic)* not including the color TV of course.

Otto looks at her. Pause. She goes on, trying to cheer herself up.

My God, the way other people act in situations like this sometimes. Kill their whole family! *(Looks at her husband)* I wish I had a movie I could show you, just the same: if you could have *seen* yourself.

Otto nods. Pause.

Well, the leopard can't change his spots, they say.

OTTO *(Nods)*: You could dive all the way down to the bottom in me like it was the ocean, go as deep as you can, you won't find any great white shark down there, you know that, don't you? *(Pause)* You think he'll come back?

MARTHA: He has the money so he's at the rock festival. When that's gone he'll get hungry and come back.

Otto looks disbelievingly at Martha. Pause.

Of course he'll come back, why shouldn't he? *(Pause)* This is his home.

OTTO: When I was little, we were out walking, and we saw this man on a horse, not a cop, a real rider. And he came toward us, my momma and me, and when he came even with us he slowed down, in case the horse kicked I guess. And he looked at us and said "Howdydo" and laughed and went on by. And then my momma told me, "That man is the son of a king!" and took my hand and we went on. *(Short pause)* Before you even get going it's all over. *(Short pause)* Sometimes I feel like they're switching me off.

Martha looks at him. Otto nods.

Work's the only thing that's still going. Because the line keeps going. But when there's a break they switch us off. They switch us on at seven so we can work till a quarter to nine. They don't switch us off between quarter to nine and nine, they let us stand around and talk to each other and grab a snack, make plans. Then from nine till a quarter to twelve it goes again. Quarter to twelve to one they let us go to the canteen 'cause it's still part of the plant.

MARTHA: You're off your head . . .

OTTO: Then it goes on again till five, or seven if there's overtime. Right before the weekend they finally switch us off, like the electric typewriters, slip a cover over us so we don't get dusty. Then we just sit there in the hall. Three-hundred fifty men. If you got a chair, you sit on it, otherwise whatever, or sleep standing up like a horse. There's this one guy in central control who takes over from the others and plugs all our brains into the same circuit, so inside our heads, we see ourselves driving home in our own car to our families and our kids, our nice apartment, where everything's just fine and it's the weekend, just like we've been looking forward to all week: and it keeps on going that way, because now we're switched on to home we can switch on the TV. *(He laughs at the thought)* And then maybe somebody on the TV switches on the TV, eh? *(Laughs again)*

MARTHA: What are you talking about?

OTTO: "A man, a wife, and baby too,
  They all went down to see the zoo,
  They went to where the monkeys are,
  And when they peeked between the bars—
    What'd'you think they saw?
  "A man, a wife, and baby too . . ."

MARTHA: "They all went down to see the zoo . . ." *(Laughs)*
  Idiot!

OTTO: Monday morning at seven, off come the dust covers,
  everything's back to normal, and nobody notices a thing.
  (Looks at Martha) Did you know that?

MARTHA: No I didn't, because it's all nonsense, that's why.

OTTO *(Nods)*: Because you don't go out to work like I do.

MARTHA *(Sour)*: I have enough to do taking care of the
  house.

OTTO *(Nods)*: That's imaginary, too. They just don't tell you
  'cause you'd only get upset.

MARTHA: You have a screw loose, that's what I think.

OTTO: Well, what if it was true? How can you tell unless you
  work it out for yourself? Fourteen screws for the wing-
  windows, two new ones to put into the side panels, a
  couple of days excitement on the line because the brains
  upstairs know they got to allow us a little leeway while
  we're learning our new trick. *(Pause)* When we get old
  enough, they put us all together in an old empty
  warehouse and seal it up. And then they show a two-
  hour movie about ten years of happy retirement. . . .
  That's how it ends. *(Short pause)* If I could just get back
  behind [where it's real] . . .

MARTHA: You got behind this time all right! The things you
  smashed up were real enough, take my word for it!

OTTO: You trying to keep my ideas out? You can't, you
  haven't cut the wire.

MARTHA: Oh, fine, more . . .

OTTO: At first I thought that when I grew up I'd be free. But then we got to know each other and got married.

MARTHA: Thank you very much!

OTTO *(Softly)*: Sometimes I buy a magazine and beat off, instead of coming to you.

MARTHA *(Stares)*: Well, I can't compete with that.

OTTO: No.

Pause.

MARTHA: Do I disgust you? You can just tell me, it's all right.

Pause.

OTTO *(Shakes his head "No")*: How about me?

MARTHA: No.

OTTO: Sometimes, when I've *(Very softly)* got it in my hand, I think, "It's shrinking!" And then I feel like a little kid again, and I really go at it hard.

MARTHA: It's not shrinking, you can take my word for it. *(Short pause)* You're the one that's shrinking, not it.

OTTO *(Looks at her; pause)*: Everything's all balled up. I reach for anything, it's stuck. And inside me everything's oversize and falling apart.

MARTHA: Maybe you're the one falling apart.

OTTO: Like a freeway, everything just roars on through.

MARTHA: What about me?

OTTO: Yeah, you too.

MARTHA *(After a short pause)*: After all the trouble you take.

OTTO: It's not your fault, I've got rubber gloves on, like what you wash the dishes in.

MARTHA: You have to take them off, then.

OTTO: When I was a kid I liked to sleep with a wool cap on, even in summer, 'cause it came down over my ears, and

I always thought that somebody would sneak up on me
at night and cut them off with a scissors. Momma used
to take it off me when she caught me.

Pause of three minutes duration.

MARTHA: Is that it for the true confessions?

Otto looks at her. Martha goes out of the room and gets a suitcase.

OTTO: What're you doing?
MARTHA: I'm going away, Otto, I'm leaving . . .
OTTO: Why?
MARTHA: Like I'm an animal or something, not a human
being.

Otto watches her pack.

SCENE EIGHT

Rebellion

*Martha is alone in a small room. She has just come in. Her things are
lying all over the place. She is in the midst of putting things away. She
stops while she makes herself some coffee, but it takes her a long time
because she's not used to the new stove. You can see that she is annoyed by
her inability to cope with the stove. When she finishes she sits, fighting to
keep her composure. She sips her coffee, crying quietly. Pause.*

Act Three

SCENE ONE

Demolition License

In Martha's lodging, very simply furnished. Otto sits in his coat on the only chair. Martha sits on the bed, looking at Otto. Pause.

OTTO: You come home with me if I take you?

Martha shakes her head.

I shouldn't ought to take you back anyhow. Not now.
MARTHA: No. *(Pause)* Are you doing all right?
OTTO: Yep.
MARTHA: How about Ludi?
OTTO: Him too.

Pause. Martha looks at Otto, smiles.

MARTHA: You still have the apartment?
OTTO: I'll hold on to that no matter what.

Martha smiles.

I'll never go into a rooming house, never.

Martha nods.

You're not here a lot, right?

MARTHA: No, but it does for me.

OTTO *(Looks at her. Pause)*: I'm not home much either. *(Pause)* I'm not seeing anybody, understand. But soon maybe! *(Pause)* Come home with me, I forgive you and we can . . . start over. *(Pause)* OK, we won't, then. *(Gets up to leave)*

MARTHA: Just the same as ever?

OTTO: Thank God for that.

MARTHA: Haven't changed at all?

OTTO: Maybe; none of your business.

MARTHA: That's true.

OTTO *(Actually at the door now)*: You're still my wife. If I wanted to make you do your duty, you'd have to do it.

MARTHA: You wouldn't do that.

OTTO: No. *(Pause)* Can I come around again sometime?

MARTHA: When you're in the neighborhood.

OTTO: Right. See how you're doing. Well, so long.

MARTHA: See you soon, Otto.

Otto leaves. Martha looks in the mirror.

SCENE TWO

Concrete

At the door of a barracks, a lodging for workmen in the compound of a construction firm. Inside one can hear [Turkish] voices, music, card-playing, drinking, etc. Otto in his coat, his son.

OTTO: I come to get you, we're going home.

Ludwig looks at him. Pause.

Your Momma's coming back too.

Otto and Ludwig look at each other. Pause.

This is no kind of life, here.

LUDWIG: If I like it . . .

OTTO: Living in a barracks, a place to sleep and that's it, this is what my son wants to be. You ought to be ashamed, you been brought up for something better.

Ludwig nods. Pause.

You're not of age yet, I can make you come along with me if I want to.

LUDWIG: I guess so.

OTTO: Suppose I do that? *(Looks at Ludwig. Pause)* I won't though. If a person's determined to be miserable, that's his business. *(Short pause. He looks at Ludwig)* It's more comfortable at home this way anyhow, I don't have to climb over the sofa to get to the bathroom. And the thumbtacks in the walls, no matter how many times you were told.

LUDWIG: That's right. *(Pause)*

OTTO: Come on home, you've made your point.

LUDWIG: Uh-uh.

OTTO *(Feels he's been caught out)*: Only kidding. A little trap. *(Pause)*

LUDWIG: You doing all right?

OTTO: See for yourself.

LUDWIG: How about Momma?

OTTO: She's OK too.

LUDWIG: You see her?

OTTO: Course I do, she's coming back, isn't she?

LUDWIG: Right.

Pause.

OTTO: This is an awful place.

LUDWIG: But I got a job. I'm earning a living.

OTTO *(Laughs. Pause)*: Can't take much pride in saying "My son the bricklayer." Better not even mention you.

LUDWIG: Or don't start talking in the first place.

OTTO: You getting smart with me?

Ludwig shakes his head.

That's a good thing, because the law says I'm still your father, no one can take that away from me. *(Short pause)* So, I think we've talked enough: pack your bag if you've got one and then we go. I'll give you five minutes.

LUDWIG: I'm not going.

OTTO: Then I'm going to clip you one and take you along anyway.

LUDWIG: If you hit me I'll call the others.

OTTO: You'd let them gang up on your own father?

LUDWIG: If you start anything.

OTTO: Then I guess I'll have to get a cop to help me. *(Pause)* You can have the living room to yourself, your own room, do what you like there, no questions. I'll leave the TV in there. Your territory; the bedroom and my workroom is all I need. We can share the kitchen, nobody gives any orders there. We can put it all down in writing and swear to it.

LUDWIG: What about Momma?

OTTO: To hell with her. *(Pause)* You can't leave your old dad in the lurch like this, you'll be sorry you did when I'm gone, you know that.

LUDWIG: You're not going anywhere. But I'll come and see you if you like.

OTTO: I don't need any visits from you, spare yourself the trouble. *(Leaves)*

Ludwig watches, uncertain, but goes back into the barracks.

SCENE THREE
The Little Mirror

In the apartment. The change is extraordinary: it's squeaky-clean but unoccupied. Otto has arranged it to suit himself. Since he couldn't cope with the whole apartment alone, he has moved everything he needs into one room: the kitchen. It is obvious that this is the only place life continues. He sleeps here, he's moved the TV in—everything. And the kitchen is still too large. Otto really only occupies the kitchen couch, where he sleeps. And it's only a place to sleep: everything else is far away, untouched, grand.

> *Otto sits watching the Bavarian version of "What's My Line" on TV. He talks doggedly to himself as he watches. So far as possible he should look thinner, also as if he's been to the barber.*

OTTO: "[And now it's time for Bavaria's favorite panel show,] 'Jolly Jobs,' with Robert Lembke!" "[Good evening, good evening, all. Let's see if our first contestant can puzzle our panel and 'fill the piggy'![4] Would you please give our panel their first clue?]"

I Am An Asshole.

"Excuse me, what was that again?"

I am an asshole.

"Amateur or professional?"

Hard to say: see, I studied how to be an upholsterer, [but of course there wasn't any jobs, so I went on job training,] and now I work for BMW and screw sixteen screws into the Model Five-Twenty-Five.

"You are an auto builder?"

Yep: an autoscrewinstallationist . . . a screwscrewer . . . screwologist . . . screwster.

"Are you perhaps . . . a *screwdriver*?"

How's that again?

"Mr. Lembke, is the contestant a screwdriver?"

"Yes, panel, the contestant *is* a screwdriver."

"Mr. Meier, if you'd be good enough to show the panel your hands?"

Sure, glad to. . . .

"Now let's let our viewing audience at home see a fully developed pair of screwdriver hands, this one with three fingers and the other with just two. This modification is the result of breeding. The fingers that are left are twice the size of ordinary fingers and are optimally suited to their function. Mr. Meier, I wonder if you'd be kind enough to run through the typical hand-movements related to your job?"

He cripples up his hands and mimics screwing in the screws.

"Thank you so much. Even though he didn't 'fill the piggy,' let's have a wonderful round of applause for our screwscrewing contestant!"

He applauds himself. Pause. He speaks normally to himself.

I'm a worker. *Worker!* Not a doctor, not a lawyer, not an accountant, not a cabinet minister, not a factory owner. *(Pause)* I can't get any line on myself. Funny. Whether I try to or not.

SCENE FOUR

Showing Off

Otto and Martha in a little cafe.

MARTHA: It's nice of you to come by.

OTTO: I wanted to see how you were doing, it's been two

weeks since anybody's seen you, who knows what might have happened. I almost didn't have the nerve.

MARTHA: Why?

OTTO: What if I'd run into your other guy.

Martha looks.

You like your work?

MARTHA: No, it's not much of a job, but I'll get something better when there's an opening. Selling house slippers isn't very interesting.

Pause.

OTTO: If I said come back, right now, everything will be just the same as it was, you probably still wouldn't do it, huh?

MARTHA: No.

OTTO: But if you don't like working. . . . You don't have to work when you're with me.

Martha smiles.

You don't want to change back again.

MARTHA: No.

Pause.

OTTO: You grown since we been apart and I've shrunk up. That's what's rotten. I used to be a happy man. Now I sit around at home all night and think about all kinds of things, get these crazy thoughts.

MARTHA: Why's that?

OTTO: Like for example, I convince myself I'm going blind.

MARTHA: Why should you be going blind?

OTTO (*Very dramatically*): That's what I say, but I imagine it. Then I think how it would be if I was alone in a mountain cabin, somewhere lonely way high up, and suddenly I wake up one morning and notice I'm blind, like the Count of Monte Cristo, from the shit from the eagle nest he got into his eyes, and there's nobody around and no telephone where I could tell someone what's happened to me. *(Laughs at the vision he's creating)* I can find my way around the cabin, by touch, see, but I got to get out and down, 'cause I only have food for two days. And how am I going to find my way down to the valley if I'm blind? It's certain death somewhere in the wilderness, 'cause I'll lose the path, wander off, fall off a cliff, and no one will hear me. But if I stay in the cabin, it's just as hopeless. . . . *(He laughs; short pause)* It's bad with you away.

Martha gazes at him.

You think we could ever . . . ? I know you got another guy, but. . . . It doesn't have to be right now, just sometime maybe. . . . I went to a whore. It cost fifty marks and I couldn't do a thing. I asked her could she give me half the money back. But she said no and didn't give me nothing.

MARTHA: Too bad about the money.

Otto nods.

Masturbating's cheaper.

OTTO *(Looks at her, gets her point)*: Yes. *(Pause)* Suppose we just start over from the beginning.

MARTHA: Go ahead, start.

OTTO: I mean together.

MARTHA: That's crazy and you know it.

OTTO: Just because a guy smashes up an apartment once in his life doesn't mean we got to break up.

MARTHA: No.

Pause.

OTTO: You still enjoy the work?

MARTHA: I haven't enjoyed it yet. But it's better than back home. Only sometimes at night my feet feel like overshoes full of water.

OTTO: Don't you ever think about coming back?

MARTHA: I bought a little radio, and I feel better already.

OTTO: Never even think about it?

MARTHA: Don't ask stupid questions if you can't guess the answers.

OTTO: Who is he?

MARTHA: Who?

OTTO: The one you have, the other guy, I mean.

MARTHA: A lot like you. *(Laughs)*

OTTO: I don't believe it.

MARTHA: It's true.

OTTO: Couldn't you do better than that?

MARTHA: He's married, just like me, only he didn't tell his wife what I told you.

OTTO: Where'd you meet him.

MARTHA: At work. I thought, if I'm really going to do this, I'm going to need help, or I'll go back for sure, and I was determined not to. So I made friends with him.

OTTO: You never used to talk like that.

MARTHA: That was then, now is now. Ah, yes. *(Looks at him)* If somebody spits on you, you can't do much about it, Otto. But they only get one chance.

OTTO: You bitch.

Martha looks at him.

SCENE FIVE

Myself

Otto in the kitchen, evening. He is reading.

OTTO *(To himself)*: If there was some way I could know that
you could still love me, Martha . . . if there was some
way you could know the way I really am, then I could at
least give it a try. Well, but, what *are* you? Like for
instance when I try to sit down and try to do some
reading I get all confused. I want to read because I'm
lonely, right, and I know I'm not going to get anything
straight, OK, unless I try to, like, read more, but the
longer I read the more confused I get. How people can
spend years at universities, study foreign languages. . . .
Are you coming back? No.

*He goes to the door, stands uncertain, looks out the peephole, opens
the door quickly. Pause. There's nobody there. He closes the door
again.*

Just go to bed, now, like a good boy.

SCENE SIX

Who Is Who?[5]

*Sunday afternoon. Otto has put the living room to rights. He sits there
with Ludwig. They're drinking coffee and schnapps.*

OTTO: Glad you could find your way over here for once.
LUDWIG: Well, I said I'd come.
OTTO: Unexpected pleasure. Cheers.
LUDWIG: Cheers.

They drink. Pause.

OTTO: You still planning on being a bricklayer?

LUDWIG: Yes, Poppa.

OTTO: You have any idea what that means, a lifetime of that?

LUDWIG: Work.

OTTO *(Looking at him)*: I sure would rather have seen you at the bank.

LUDWIG: Bricklayers make more than bank messengers.

OTTO: But when you're a workman, you're *nothing*. Get filthy, morning to night. You go into a tavern, the barmaid can tell just by looking at your hands, this guy don't amount to much.

LUDWIG: But you're a worker, Poppa. You didn't even go to trade school.

OTTO: So much the worse for me. You remember what you said: better dead than like me?

Ludwig nods. Pause.

Well, why do you think you said that?

LUDWIG: I didn't mean it.

OTTO: Because I'm nobody. I'm nothing to look up to.

Short pause.

LUDWIG: But . . . you don't want to be any different than you are, do you?

OTTO: I would have jumped right out of my skin and run away long ago if there was any way I could. *(Pause)* I'm not making excuses. I feel like I'm standing in a hole, and I want to climb out to where it's light, about thirty feet over my head. But there's nothing to get a grip on, it's all slick. *(Laughs)* When I've had a little too much to drink I feel like taking a razor blade and cutting myself open top to bottom, and it's as if somebody else would come climbing out of my skin, somebody who I've been all along only he's had no way to get out.

LUDWIG: Like the frog-prince.

OTTO: Are you making fun of your father?

LUDWIG: No.

OTTO: It doesn't matter. I just wish you didn't have to go through that. A man needs something he can recognize himself by, something to be proud of. *(Pause)* The Average Man.

LUDWIG [*(Nervously joking)*]: You're not average, Poppa; you're smaller than average.

OTTO [*(Taking the remark seriously)*]: Maybe 'cause I didn't grow to where I was supposed to.

LUDWIG: What's that supposed to mean?

OTTO: If all you are's a bricklayer, Ludi, I wish you the very best, but you're going to find out you're no different from me and you'll remember what I said. Sometime you're going to look around and see just what a bricklayer amounts to in this world, and that's nothing, and that there are so many other things in the world! *(Nods)* And then you're going to be exactly like I am now, I guarantee you.

LUDWIG: No I won't.

Otto smiles.

Poppa, I don't just want to be a bricklayer, I want to be a human being.

Pause.

OTTO: Maybe so.

Pause.

LUDWIG: What's holding you back from being who you want to be, if you're not satisfied the way things are?

OTTO: Dreams.

LUDWIG: Right. Poor Poppa.

OTTO: You know about that, do you? About having conversations with yourself?

LUDWIG: No.

OTTO: I do. I think things up that way. *(Laughs)*

LUDWIG: Like, you pretend you're rich?

OTTO: Not so much rich as recognized . . . successful.

LUDWIG: But if you had your weight in gold . . .

OTTO *(Laughs)*: Like the Aga Khan . . .

LUDWIG: . . . you'd still be the same person.

OTTO: But money makes a difference!

Ludwig looks at his father.

You know, I often thought that I'd trade all the years I got left for just one, if . . .

LUDWIG: What would you do?

OTTO: God . . . just to be four or five inches taller, and handsome, have all the women checking me out, and if I liked one all I'd have to do is smile at her and off she'd go with me, love me; and lots of friends, because I'm rich and throw my money around, take trips around the world and if anyone wants to come along, they're welcome; no grief, no loneliness, no trouble—just freedom.

LUDWIG: And what happens when the year's over?

OTTO: It'd be a long year. *(Short pause)* I went to a whore a while back. I shouldn't tell you something like that, but now it doesn't matter.

LUDWIG: That's disgusting.

OTTO *(Laughs)*: Your Momma doesn't want me anymore. A person's got to look out for himself. She's got herself another man, your mother has.

LUDWIG: What if you went to see her?

OTTO: She boots me out.

LUDWIG: Have you been there already?
OTTO: Yeah. Before I lost my nerve . . .
LUDWIG: How come?
OTTO: 'Cause he's always there.

Pause.

LUDWIG: I got to go now.

Otto looks at him. Ludwig stands up.

OTTO: You can stay ten more minutes.

SCENE SEVEN

Farewell

In Martha's room. After sex, Otto and Martha both in bed. They talk very softly.

OTTO: You got two men now. *(Short pause)* But I don't have two women.
MARTHA: Find yourself another.
OTTO: None of 'em'll have me except you.
MARTHA: Likely story.
OTTO: Cross my heart.
MARTHA: They don't know what's good for them.
OTTO: I'm stuck with you. S'awful.
MARTHA: Idiot.

Pause.

OTTO: Does he know that I come around here?
MARTHA: Of course, I told him.
OTTO: What'd he say?
MARTHA: What could he say, he's married too, I already told you that.

Pause.

OTTO: How does he do it?

MARTHA: Do what?

OTTO: From behind, or . . .

MARTHA: Don't talk that way, Otto.

OTTO: Like me, or sophisticated?

MARTHA: Stop it.

OTTO: Like me?

MARTHA: Yes.

OTTO: Bitch.

MARTHA: What?

OTTO: Bitch.

Pause.

MARTHA: You haven't changed the least little bit.

OTTO: You protected me; now I'm naked.

MARTHA: Unfortunately.

OTTO: And now it's too late.

MARTHA: Let's talk about something else. How's everything at the plant?

OTTO: Bad, just like always.

MARTHA: You always look at the dark side of everything.

OTTO: What I'd really like is to crawl right up inside you and never come out. Like a baby, you know?

Martha laughs.

You just pull me in right in there and I'm gone.

Martha laughs.

So how's it been with you?

MARTHA: Next month I get transferred to another department.

OTTO: Not a brain in her head. That's not the kind of thing I mean!

MARTHA: Well, it's important to me!

OTTO: You never feel like you want to come back home?

MARTHA: Of course I do, sometimes.

OTTO: I need you.

MARTHA: Oh, nonsense. You're a tidy man and don't need much picking up after. And Ludi, toward the end he was like a little mouse, he would have washed his own underwear if I'd've let him. But when nobody's at home, housework is stupid.

OTTO: You've got a bad conscience, haven't you, woman?

MARTHA: Wouldn't that just suit you. There used to be whole mornings when I sat down and howled like a barnyard dog. Not *about* anything; there wasn't anything to cry about; but just the same I'd finish the housework, sit down at the kitchen table and wait for the tears to come: can you understand that? *(Laughs)* It'd really give them something to talk about at the store if I sat down and started bawling. But I don't need to anymore, because I have a living to earn.

OTTO: There isn't any sweetness left in you. You talk like a man.

MARTHA: Then find yourself a woman to talk to.

OTTO: Don't you have any respect for me anymore? No, because the other one, he's better than me, isn't he?

MARTHA: If you go on talking like that, Otto, I promise you this is the last time you'll ever lie in my bed.

Otto laughs. Pause.

OTTO: Suppose I changed so much you'd never know me?

Martha looks at him.

You'd like that, wouldn't you?

MARTHA: I'm getting up now.

She does. Otto watches her.

SCENE EIGHT

Man

Otto alone in the kitchen, late at night. He has had too much to drink, looks sloppy besides. He has a book in one hand, his finger marking his place.

OTTO *(To himself)*: I have this longing, Martha. I see myself
from a long way off. My skin is tanned, I'm doing heavy
work and I'm sweating. Suddenly you come running,
you're looking for me. When you see me you come up to
me, you want to say something. Then you suddenly
jump back like you're frightened. My eyes are calm, I got
a handsome face, not stupid or afraid. But it's me, all
right.

When he stops talking, his expression is strange and vacant. He pages through the book a little. Then he opens his trousers and starts to masturbate, weakly and without pleasure. After a little while tears begin to run down his face. He cries.

SCENE NINE

The End

In Martha's rooming-house room [a different one]. Martha and Ludwig are hugging each other.

MARTHA: Did your Poppa send you?

Ludwig shakes his head "No."

I haven't seen you for so long.
LUDWIG: Because you went underground.

MARTHA *(Laughs)*: I had to move, your father wouldn't leave me alone for five minutes.

LUDWIG: Don't you ever go home?

Martha shakes her head "No."

Me either. *(Pause. He looks around)*

MARTHA: It's not the kind of life you dream about, is it? But an old lady like me . . .

LUDWIG: Who says you're an old lady?

MARTHA: The employment office, that's who: an old lady with no training and no experience. If the department store hadn't taken me on in the shoe department . . .

Ludwig laughs.

All day long I sell house slippers, can you imagine? I have my own table that I'm responsible for. They don't let me near the cash register yet. But that'll come when I've shown I can do the work. *(Pause)* Sometimes I feel like dropping everything and just going home.

LUDWIG: If you did I'd go too.

MARTHA *(Nods)*: When I'm at the end of my strength because I don't seem able to do something or other. *(Laughs)* It's not as if it's hard work. All I have is my one table to stand behind, fuss with the merchandise so it looks tidy; "salesworthy" the manager says. When somebody asks me something I answer them, when they buy something I wrap it and take it to the cashier. If I sell a lot I go to the basement and bring up more. Once a month they give me new styles . . . *(She starts to cry)*

LUDWIG: Go home, Momma.

MARTHA: People like me should stay where they're put. I didn't realize that. Sometimes I stand there and just shake from head to foot. *(Pause)* I'm not used to it. That's what it is. It ought to be so simple. Not even sizes are a problem, not with house slippers; half a size bigger than your street shoe, that's all. *(Smiles)* And in the evening I sit here as if I've been running a marathon all day. *(Pause)* And then your father comes and wants to argue for hours when I'm dead tired and have other things to think about. Not now, because he doesn't have my new address yet. *(Smiles)* And if you give it to him, you'll be sorry, young man. . . .

Ludwig shakes his head "I won't."

I even told him I have another beau, just so he'd leave me in peace. *(Smiles)*

LUDWIG: Is it true?

MARTHA: Don't be silly, you think I'd get involved again so fast?

Ludwig laughs, relieved.

And what about you, are you satisfied?

LUDWIG: Better than before, anyhow.

Martha smiles, nods.

Didn't you ever love Poppa?

MARTHA: Oh, honey, what does that mean? I put up with him, those last few years. That's perfectly normal.

LUDWIG: But not love.

MARTHA: Who knows. . . . Let's talk about something else. *(Laughs)* You know I can't stand to look at a pair of slippers? Not even the pair I brought from home and . . .

LUDWIG: And didn't steal from the store? *(Laughs)*

MARTHA: Idiot. *(Pause)* If everything goes right, I'm supposed to be transferred to another department, that's what they promised me. To housewares. That's what I'm hoping for, because I think I'll feel better where things are more interesting.

LUDWIG: My work is interesting already.

MARTHA: Because you're learning something. That's the difference.

Pause. She wipes away the tears of earlier.

LUDWIG: Don't, Momma . . .

MARTHA *(Nods)*: I won't. Sorry to be so mushy. *(Pause)* Just yesterday I went to the movies. The first time. And do you know what happened? After the show, while I was looking at the pictures in the lobby, a man my own age came up to me and asked me if I'd like a bite to eat! *(Smiles)* Of course I didn't say a word and walked right away . . .

LUDWIG: Good thing you did.

MARTHA: He was very nice-looking.

LUDWIG: Let's move in together.

Martha smiles.

I can't stay where I am now. The company's supposed to keep it for foreign workers, and you got to be eighteen for them to make an exception.

MARTHA: You've got courage, that's a good thing.

LUDWIG: Hold out your hand.

Martha does. Ludwig squeezes it hard.

MARTHA: Ow!

LUDWIG *(Laughs)*: That's right. *(Pause)* Either we move in together or I give your new address to Poppa. *(Laughs)*

MARTHA: Blackmailer. *(Pause)* Maybe in a few more months, when we've all found out how to stand on our own feet. I can't bother myself about you right now, Ludi. I have to think about myself first, and I'm not used to that.

LUDWIG: What about Poppa?

MARTHA *(Shrugs her shoulders, calmly)*: He has to do the same.

LUDWIG: What?

MARTHA: Just the same as us. He has to learn.

NOTES

1 The script does not spell it out, but the implication is that the fellow worker who returned the pen is a Turkish or South Italian *Gastarbeiter* and hence by nature dishonest. Martha's final line actually reads, "To err is human." The change brings the racial motif a little closer to the surface. If desired, Otto's "One of them . . ." can be made explicit; "One of them Turks/Eyetyes/Greasers/Darkies/etc."

2 The forgotten items in Otto's accounting are actually "Radi," the giant white radishes that many Bavarians relish with their beer. In order to avoid distracting an American audience with folkloric irrelevancies, "the radish-seller" has become "the pretzel girl."

3 Scene title in English in original.

4 In this passage Otto uses various "voices" for the moderator and panelists. *Heitere Berufraten* (literally, "Amusing Job-Guessing") uses "coins" in a piggy bank to indicate a contestant's score instead of flip cards à la *What's My Line*: hence "fill the piggy."

5 Scene title in English in original.

THE PLAYS OF FRANZ XAVER KROETZ

1970

*Game Crossing; Piecework; Michi's Blood; Hard as Nails;
Men's Business*

1971

Barnyard; Dark Ride; Dear Fritz; Request Concert; Inconclusive

1972

*Global Interests; Lienz, City in the Dolomites; Upper
Austria; Maria Magdalena* (adapted from Hebbel)

1973

Munich Born; A Vote for Life

1974

Pennies from Heaven; The Nest; Broader Prospects

1975

Road to Happiness; Homeland

1976

Through the Leaves; All the Best from Grado; Agnes Bernauer
(adapted from Hebbel)

1977
Mensch Meier; Tales of the Chiemgau

1979
Good Ol' Max

1982
Neither Fish nor Fowl

1983
Fear and Hope in the FRG

1985
Farmers Die; The Gelded Boar (adapted from Toller)

1991
Farmer Theater

FRANZ XAVER KROETZ was born in Munich, West Germany in 1946. He attended acting school and worked in various alternative theatres (including the late Rainer Werner Fassbinder's *antiteater*) during the Sixties. His first experiments in playwrighting were influenced by the realistic, socially-critical plays of ordinary life written in the 1920s and '30s by Ödön von Horvath and Marie-luise Fleisser, but Kroetz began to find his own distinctive voice in 1970, after receiving a stipend from the Suhrkamp publishing house which allowed him to write plays fulltime. Since then he has written more than 30 plays, radio scripts and television plays. By 1973 he had become Germany's most-produced living play-wright, but his first widespread popular and financial success was the family drama *Mensch Meier*, which had its world premiere in four simultaneous productions in 1978. A militant communist in the mid-1970s, Kroetz became a German television star in 1988 by appearing in *Kir Royal*, a popular miniseries. His most recent play, *Farmer Theater*, was produced in 1991.

A previous volume of Kroetz plays in English, *Farmyard and Four Other Plays*, was published by Urizen Books in 1976. The first production in the United States to receive widespread atten-tion was the JoAnne Akalaitis / Joan MacIntosh *Request Concert* at Women's Interart Theater in New York in 1981. Subsequent

American productions have included stagings by Empty Space Theater in Seattle, Washington; L.A. Theatre Works; Manhattan Theater Club; and Mabou Mines at the New York Shakespeare Festival's Public Theater.

THE TRANSLATOR

ROGER DOWNEY first encountered the German language as a child in the home of his East Prussian grandfather and Swiss grandmother. Two years of study at the University of Chicago and two and a half years residence in Frankfurt am Main with the U.S. Army improved the acquaintance. His first translation (Georg Büchner's *Woyzeck*) was made in 1975 for the Empty Space. Since then he has translated plays by Lessing, Kleist, Ödön von Horvath, and Frank Wedekind as well as those of Franz Xaver Kroetz contained in this volume. In more recent years he has expanded his horizons to plays from the French and Russian repertories. Since 1976 he has served as senior editor and theatre critic of the Seattle *Weekly*.

CPSIA information can be obtained
at www.ICGtesting.com
Printed in the USA
JSHW061811191222
35156JS00001B/59